Contents

KV-466-001

Criminal Justice

London: H M S O

Researched and written by Publishing Services,
Central Office of Information.

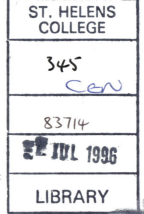

HMSO

HMSO publications are available from:

HMSO Publications Centre
(Mail, fax and telephone orders only)
PO Box 276, London SW8 5DT
Telephone orders 0171 873 9090
General enquiries 0171 873 0011
(queuing system in operation for both numbers)
Fax orders 0171 873 8200

HMSO Bookshops
49 High Holborn, London WC1V 6HB
(counter service only)
0171 873 0011   Fax 0171 831 1326
68–69 Bull Street, Birmingham B4 6AD
0121 236 9696 Fax 0121 236 9699
33 Wine Street, Bristol BS1 2BQ
0117 9264306   Fax 0117 9294515
9–21 Princess Street, Manchester M60 8AS
0161 834 7201   Fax 0161 833 0634
16 Arthur Street, Belfast BT1 4GD
01232 238451   Fax 01232 235401
71 Lothian Road, Edinburgh EH3 9AZ
0131 228 4181   Fax 0131 229 2734
The HMSO Oriel Bookshop
The Friary, Cardiff CF1 4AA
01222 395548   Fax 01222 384347

HMSO's Accredited Agents
(see Yellow Pages)

and through good booksellers

Introduction

Although Britain[1] is a unitary state, there are three systems of criminal justice—one in England and Wales, one in Scotland and one in Northern Ireland. There are a number of differences in both law and practice in Scotland and, to a lesser extent, Northern Ireland, although the general policy objectives are the same as those for England and Wales. For example, Scotland has a different court and prosecution system and, like Northern Ireland, has separate prison and police services. These and other significant variations are described in this book.

The criminal law—which is concerned with acts punishable by the state—is interpreted by the courts, but changes in the law are normally matters for Parliament as the supreme legislative authority. If a court reaches a decision which is contrary to the intentions of Parliament, Parliament must either accept the decision or pass amending legislation. Most legislation affecting criminal law is government-sponsored, usually in consultation with interested parties, such as the police, the legal profession, the probation service and voluntary bodies.

The effectiveness of the system in England and Wales was examined by a Royal Commission on Criminal Justice between 1991 and 1993 and a number of significant recommendations for change were made. Some of these were addressed by the Criminal Justice and Public Order Act which, together with the Police and

---

[1] The term 'Britain' is used informally in this book to mean the United Kingdom of Great Britain and Northern Ireland; 'Great Britain' comprises England, Scotland and Wales.

Magistrates' Courts Act, formed a major part of the Government's legislative programme in 1994.

Further important legislation introducing a Criminal Cases Review Commission in England, Wales and Northern Ireland (see p. 51), and enhancing the powers of the criminal justice agencies in Scotland, was enacted in July 1995.

Although every attempt has been made to ensure that this book is accurate and up to date, it should not be regarded as offering a definitive view on legal matters.

Crime

Trends and Statistics

Differences in the legal systems, police recording practices and statistical classifications in the countries of Britain make it impracticable to analyse in detail trends in crime for the country as a whole. Nevertheless, it is clear that, as in Western Europe generally, there has been a substantial increase in crime since the early 1950s. Annual official statistics cover only crime recorded by the police and can be affected by changes in the proportion of crimes which are undiscovered or unreported.

Table 1: Notifiable Offences Recorded by the Police in England and Wales in 1994

Offence Group	Recorded crimes (thousands)	Crimes cleared up (thousands)	(per cent)
Violence against the person	219.7	168.5	(77)
Sexual offences	32.0	24.4	(76)
Burglary	1,261.4	268.9	(21)
Robbery	60.0	13.1	(22)
Theft and handling stolen goods	2,560.7	606.7	(24)
Fraud and forgery	146.2	75.6	(52)
Criminal damage	930.4	123.6[a]	(17)[a]
Other	47.7	45.7	(96)
Total	5,258.1	1,326.5	(26)

Source: *Criminal Statistics England and Wales 1994.*

[a] Excludes criminal damage at £20 or under.

In 1994 the Scottish police recorded 527,064 crimes, of which 195,745 were cleared up. In addition, there were 463,917 lesser statutory offences, most of which were connected with motoring. In Northern Ireland 67,886 crimes were recorded in 1994, of which 24,342 were cleared up.

About 94 per cent of offences recorded by the police in England and Wales are directed against property—homes, vehicles and buildings—and only 6 per cent involve violence. Rising affluence has provided more opportunities for casual property crime. In 1957, for example, car crime was only one-tenth of total crime but this has risen in 1994 to about 28 per cent. Crime tends to be concentrated in large cities and urban areas. The demand for, and supply of, illegal drugs has been an increasing factor in the incidence of crime in recent years.

Regular crime surveys are undertaken in England and Wales and in Scotland. These indicate that many crimes go unrecorded by the police, mainly because not all victims report what has happened to them. The surveys confirm that the majority of crimes are against property, in the form of theft and vandalism.

Most crime is committed by young males, is opportunist and is not planned by hardened professional criminals, although these do exist. There are about eight times as many male offenders as female. Only a small proportion of young male offenders go on to become serious repeat offenders.

Prevention

About 800 specialist crime prevention officers are employed in police forces across England and Wales. The Home Office provides support to the police effort through its Crime Prevention Centre, which offers training and advice and disseminates best practice.

At a national level, 12 government departments are represented on the Ministerial Group on Crime Prevention, which is chaired by a Home Office Minister. The Group co-ordinates national action and helps to ensure that government departments pursue crime prevention objectives in the implementation of their own policies.

Partners Against Crime

A major initiative promoting co-operation between the public and the police—Partners Against Crime—was launched by the Government in September 1994. It is based on a three-tier approach:

1. There are already 142,000 Neighbourhood Watch schemes in England and Wales covering over 5 million households. There are also some 3,600 schemes in Scotland. Residents keep an eye on properties in their area and pass on to the police information about people or vehicles which arouse their suspicions.

2. Street Watch is separate from Neighbourhood Watch. Local people, in agreement with the police, work out specific routes and regularly walk the chosen area. They use their eyes and ears to help the police, and also offer support to the elderly and vulnerable.

3. The Neighbourhood Constable scheme is a variation of the existing special constabulary (see p. 13). Like special constables, neighbourhood constables are police-trained, uniformed volunteers with the full range of police powers, but they work in their own neighbourhood. It is anticipated that 3,000 of these constables will be on patrol by the end of 1996.

Safer Cities Programme

The Government's Safer Cities Programme tackles crime and the fear of crime in inner city and urban areas in England through joint action by local government, private businesses, the police and voluntary agencies. Twenty locally-based projects had by October 1994 supported 3,600 schemes with funding of over £22 million. Some of these projects, having completed their remit, have been succeeded by multi-agency community safety bodies. The second phase of the programme has seen the establishment of 32 new projects, including some in Wales.

There is a Safer Cities programme in Scotland, and similar projects are being funded by the Government in Northern Ireland.

Other Initiatives

Some 1,300 local crime prevention panels (including 900 mainly school-based youth panels) assist the police in preventing crime through publicity, marking goods and equipment, and fund-raising to buy security devices.

Crime Concern, a national independent organisation, encourages local initiatives and business participation in crime prevention.

In 1994 the Home Office issued a booklet on best practice in the use of closed-circuit television (CCTV) for the prevention and investigation of crime; the Government has actively encouraged the setting up of CCTV schemes across the country, especially in town centres.

The National Board for Crime Prevention, set up in 1993, advises the Government about ways of involving all sections of the community in the development and delivery of crime prevention in England and Wales. There is also a Scottish Crime Prevention Council and a Northern Ireland Crime Prevention Panel.

Supporting the Victim

The Government has emphasised the importance of victims' interests within the criminal justice system.

There are some 365 victim support schemes—with some 12,000 volunteer visitors, covering the whole of England and Wales—providing practical help and emotional support to victims of crime. They are co-ordinated by a national organisation, Victim Support, which receives a government grant (£10.8 million in 1995–96). Most of the grant goes to local schemes to meet either the salaries of the staff who organise the volunteers, or scheme running costs. Similar schemes operate in Scotland and Northern Ireland. Government support for Victim Support Scotland in 1995–96 is almost £1 million.

In England and Wales the Witness Service, run by Victim Support with Home Office funding, provides support for victims and witnesses attending the Crown Court. About 55 witness schemes have been set up to help victims through the stress of giving evidence; the Witness Service is being extended to all 78 main Crown Court centres by the end of 1995.

A new offence of witness intimidation was introduced by the Criminal Justice and Public Order Act 1994 to protect victims who are also witnesses. The same legislation provides for the abolition of committal proceedings (see p. 41), so that victims no longer have to give evidence and be cross-examined twice over.

The Government accepted all the recommendations made by the Royal Commission on Criminal Justice in 1993 on help for the victims of crime, such as giving them better information about the progress of investigations or court proceedings and improving facilities for them at court. Most of these have now been implemented, and the 50 standards of treatment set out in the Victims' Charter (published by the Government in 1990) have been or are well on the way to being met (see also Courts Charter—p. 43).

In September 1994 the Government announced that reports prepared on offenders before sentencing would include a section about the effects of the crime on the victim (see p. 50).

Compensation

The Criminal Injuries Compensation Scheme, applicable in England, Wales and Scotland, provides compensation for personal injury resulting from crimes of violence. It paid out £170 million in 1994–95. In Northern Ireland there are separate statutory arrangements for compensation for criminal injuries, and for malicious damage to property, including any resulting loss of profits. Nearly £90 million was paid out under those arrangements in 1994–95.

Britain is a party to a European Convention under which mutual arrangements for compensation apply to citizens of those countries in which the Convention is in force.

Strengthening the Law

Important measures to strengthen the criminal justice system have been taken in recent years. The courts, for instance, have powers to trace, freeze and confiscate the proceeds of drug trafficking. A court can require an offender to pay an amount equal to the full value of the proceeds arising from the trafficking. Following a conviction, the onus is on the offender to prove that property does not represent the proceeds of trafficking. Offenders may not opt to serve a period of imprisonment in default of paying a confiscation order. Restraint and confiscation orders made by courts can be enforced against assets held overseas, and vice versa, if a bilateral confiscation agreement has been made between Britain and another state.

A court in England, Wales and Northern Ireland may also confiscate the proceeds of offences such as robbery, fraud, blackmail and insider dealing in shares. These powers are being strengthened by the Proceeds of Crime Act 1995, which contains measures to:

—make convicted criminals account for the legal origin of all their property, and confiscate it if they cannot;

—give the authorities stronger asset tracing powers to deal with the concealment of criminal assets; and

—confiscate proceeds which come to light up to six years after conviction.

The Criminal Justice (Scotland) Act 1995 (most provisions of which are being implemented on 1 April 1996) introduces powers for the courts in Scotland to order confiscation of the proceeds of general crime and widens their powers for ordering forfeiture.

New powers to clamp down on money launderers[2] came into force in 1994, with heavy penalties for those who launder money gained from any sort of serious crime.

There are strict legislative controls on firearms. The police license the possession of firearms and have powers to regulate their safekeeping and movement. The private ownership of certain highly dangerous types of weapon, such as machine guns, high-

[2] Money laundering is the process by which illegally obtained property—from drugs or arms trafficking, terrorist activities or other serious crimes—is given the appearance of having originated from a legitimate source.

powered self-loading rifles and burst-fire weapons, is banned. New laws for Northern Ireland against imitation firearms took effect in December 1994.

It is unlawful to manufacture, sell or import certain weapons, such as knuckledusters, or to carry a knife in a public place without good reason.

The Criminal Justice Act 1991 made a number of reforms to the criminal law in England and Wales, mainly concerning sentencing and the system for early release of prisoners (see p. 73). Similar reforms in Scotland took effect from October 1993 under the Prisoners and Criminal Proceedings (Scotland) Act 1993.

The Police and Magistrates' Courts Act 1994 and the Criminal Justice and Public Order Act 1994 (mainly applicable in England and Wales, but also to some extent in Scotland) are designed to improve the organisation and management of the police, so that they are better able to combat crime, and to tilt the balance of the criminal justice system further against criminals.

The Criminal Justice (Scotland) Act 1995 increases the capacity of the criminal justice system in Scotland to deal with offenders, and increases the powers available to prevent crime and reduce re-offending.

Measures to Combat Terrorism

Certain special powers are available to assist in preventing and investigating terrorist crime. The powers take account of the need to maintain a proper balance between the safety of the public and the rights of the individual. They must be renewed by Parliament each year and the use of the powers is reviewed annually by an independent person.

The Prevention of Terrorism (Temporary Provisions) Act 1989 applies throughout Britain. It makes it unlawful to support specified organisations involved in terrorism connected with the affairs of Northern Ireland, and enables the Government to exclude from all or part of Britain people who are believed to be involved in such terrorism. The legislation also gives the police wider powers to deal with suspected terrorists, including international terrorists, than are available under the general criminal law. For example, the police may arrest terrorist suspects without warrant and hold them for up to 48 hours, and ministerial approval may be sought to extend detention for up to a further five days. There are also special powers for the police to conduct security checks at ports and airports.

The 1989 Act contains strong powers to deal with those who provide financial support for terrorism, or who launder terrorist funds, including powers to order the restraint or forfeiture of terrorist funds. The legislation allows for reciprocal enforcement arrangements with other countries.

The Criminal Justice and Public Order Act 1994 gives the police new powers to stop and search for articles which may be used for terrorist purposes, and creates a new offence of possession of such articles.

The Government maintains that there should be no concessions to terrorist demands and that international co-operation is essential in tracking down terrorists and impeding their movement between countries.

Northern Ireland

The security forces in Northern Ireland have special powers to search, question and arrest under the Northern Ireland

(Emergency Provisions) Act 1991. A person who is detained under emergency provisions is entitled to consult a solicitor privately.

The ceasefires declared by the paramilitary groupings in Northern Ireland in 1994 have led to a new security situation, but the Government does not think it would be prudent to remove the protection of the emergency legislation from the statute book while there are still illegal weaponry and explosives at large.

The Police and Their Powers

The Home Secretary and the Scottish and Northern Ireland Secretaries, together with police authorities and chief constables, are responsible for the provision of an effective and efficient police service in Britain.

Organisation

There are 52 police forces in Britain, mainly organised on a local basis: 43 in England and Wales, eight in Scotland and one (the Royal Ulster Constabulary) in Northern Ireland. The Metropolitan Police Force and the City of London force are responsible for policing London. In addition, the British Transport Police are responsible for policing the railway network, including the London Underground and Docklands Light Railway; the Ministry of Defence Police are responsible chiefly for the policing of military establishments in Great Britain; and the United Kingdom Atomic Energy Authority Constabulary is responsible for policing nuclear establishments and for escorting nuclear material between establishments. The police service is financed by central and local government.

At the end of 1994 police strength in Britain was about 150,000, of which the Metropolitan Police numbered over 28,000. The establishment of the Royal Ulster Constabulary was around 8,500. Police strength in Scotland was 14,300.

Each force has volunteer special constables who perform police duties in their spare time, without pay, acting in support of regular officers. The special constabulary symbolises the links that exist between police forces and the communities they serve. The Government is aiming to recruit a further 10,000 special constables by the end of 1996, so increasing the overall number by 50 per cent. In Northern Ireland there is a 5,000-strong part-time and full-time paid reserve.

Police forces are maintained in England and Wales by local police authorities (see p. 15). The Home Secretary is responsible for London's Metropolitan Police Force. The police authorities in Scotland are the regional and islands councils, although new unitary councils will assume this role from April 1996. The Royal Ulster Constabulary is responsible to a police authority appointed by the Secretary of State for Northern Ireland.

Provincial forces are headed by chief constables. They are generally answerable to the police authorities for their force's competence, efficiency and conduct. The police authorities appoint the chief constable and assistant chief constable. They also fix the maximum strength of the force, and provide buildings and equipment (although not in Scotland until April 1996). London's Metropolitan Police Commissioner and immediate subordinates are appointed on the recommendation of the Home Secretary.

Police officers are not allowed to join a trade union or to go on strike. All ranks, however, have their own staff associations.

Inspectorates of Constabulary

Police forces are subject to inspection by independent Inspectorates of Constabulary reporting to central government. There are two inspectorates—one for England, Wales and Northern Ireland, and the other for Scotland. The aims of the inspections are to:

—assess the effectiveness and efficiency of forces;

—influence the development of policing which meets community needs; and

—disseminate examples of good practice to police forces.

The inspectors consist of former police officers and lay experts with a range of professional experience outside the police service. Reports of all major inspections are published. Both inspectorates publish annual reports covering the whole range of police matters.

Reforms

The Police and Magistrates' Courts Act 1994 gives effect to proposals for police reform set out in a Government White Paper published in June 1993, and to proposals on police responsibilities and rewards which were announced by the Home Secretary in October 1993 and which required primary legislation.

The Act is designed to change the relationship between central government, police authorities and chief constables—to improve the management of the police and to reduce cumbersome central controls, devolving more power and decision-making to the local level.

Police Authorities

The legislation provides for the appointment of independent members to police authorities in England and Wales outside London, in addition to local councillors and magistrates. The standard size of a police authority is set at 17 members, comprising nine locally elected councillors, three magistrates and five independent members. The Home Secretary may increase the size of an authority beyond 17 if local circumstances make it desirable. The independent members are chosen by the other members of the police authority, from a list of ten names forwarded by the Home Secretary from a short-list of 20 prepared by a local selection panel. A new 12-member Metropolitan Police Committee assists the Home Secretary, who acts as police authority for the Metropolitan Police.

Police authorities in Scotland continue to be composed of elected councillors.

Other Provisions

Other main provisions of the legislation include:

—setting key objectives for the police by the Government, which prioritise the fighting of crime and the protection of the public. In 1995–96 these objectives are: increasing detection rates for violent crime and burglaries, providing high visibility policing to reassure the public, responding promptly to emergency calls, and targeting crimes which are a particular local problem (including drug-related criminality), in partnership with the public and local agencies;

—setting local policing objectives by police authorities, in consultation with the chief constables and local community;

—placing a greater emphasis on community needs through published annual local policing plans, prepared by the chief constable and agreed by the police authority, and published annual reports setting out achievements against the plans;

—strengthening the role of the Inspectorate of Constabulary, which assumes a statutory responsibility to inspect the Metropolitan Police;

—ending detailed government controls on finance and manpower from April 1995 by giving chief constables new freedom to manage police and civilian staff and to determine staff numbers; and

—introducing fixed-term appointments for senior police officers from April 1995 and abolishing the ranks of deputy chief constable and chief superintendent.

The duties of the police in Scotland have been set out in statute for many years.

Co-ordination of Police Operations

Certain police services are provided centrally either by the Government or through co-operation between forces. In England and Wales these include criminal intelligence, telecommunications, and research and development. In Scotland the main common services are centralised police training, the Scottish Crime Squad and the Scottish Criminal Record Office.

The National Criminal Intelligence Service, with a headquarters in London and five regional offices, co-ordinates and provides information to the police and HM Customs about major criminals and organised crime, including drug trafficking. The Service also liaises with the International Criminal Police Organisation (INTERPOL), which promotes international co-operation between police forces.

Britain has taken the lead in developing, with other European Union members, a European police organisation (EUROPOL) designed to provide Union-wide intelligence about serious crime. The Convention on EUROPOL was signed by member states in July 1995.

All British police forces have fraud squads responsible for investigating financial and commercial fraud.

Six regional crime squads in England and Wales deal with serious crime which goes beyond individual force, regional or national boundaries.

The Police National Computer provides all British police forces with rapid 24-hour-a-day access to operationally essential information. Phoenix—the Criminal Justice Record Service—is being implemented on the Police National Computer, and will give the police direct on-screen access to national records of arrests, bail decisions, and convictions. This will gradually replace the manual record-keeping service currently operated by the National Identification Bureau (NIB), which is located at Metropolitan Police headquarters but financed by all police forces. Phoenix will eventually provide information direct to other agencies, such as the courts, the Prison Service and the Crown Prosecution Service.

The Police National Network, a new communications network providing the full range of telecommunications services to forces throughout Britain, was officially opened in November 1994.

Scottish criminal records are held on computer at the Scottish Criminal Record Office, which has an automatic national finger-print record system. The initial implementation of a similar national system in England and Wales is planned for 1997–98.

The Police National Missing Persons Bureau, which comes under the NIB, was launched in March 1994. It is the first national database of missing people, holding information which all forces and international agencies can share.

Recognising the need for an information systems strategy for the police, the Government launched the first national blueprint for police use of computer technology in November 1994. The National Strategy for Police Information Systems sets out the importance of sharing data and buying compatible systems.

Forensic Science Service

The Forensic Science Service (FSS) serves the administration of justice in England and Wales by providing scientific support in the investigation of crime, and by giving evidence to the courts. Its customers include the police, the Crown Prosecution Service (see p. 39), coroners and defence solicitors.

In February 1995 the Government announced that the FSS would merge with the Metropolitan Police Forensic Science Laboratory with effect from April 1996 to form a single agency serving all police forces in England and Wales through seven regional operational laboratories.

In Scotland forensic science services are provided by forces' own laboratories. Northern Ireland has its own forensic science laboratory.

Casework

Scientific expertise is available on a case-by-case basis to overseas law enforcement agencies and attorneys. The Forensic Science Service provides assistance to overseas police forces in the investigation of many crimes, particularly fires where arson is suspected, cases involving DNA profiling and offences involving the use of firearms.

The scientists have a wide range of experience in fire scene examination, including fatal fires in domestic premises, large industrial fires and vehicle fires.

DNA profiling is a revolutionary scientific testing process which can positively identify an individual from a specimen of blood, semen, hair roots or tissue. Its application to crime specimens represents the greatest advance in forensic science in decades. Initial laboratory work took place at the University of Leicester, and extensive research work by Home Office scientists led to refinement and extension of the technique so that it could be used on forensic samples. The vast potential of DNA profiling is recognised by the police and the legal profession, and its use in criminal investigation has increased (see also p. 33).

The FSS provides advice on firearms and related matters and assistance in the investigation of shooting incidents. When presented with a suspect weapon, the expert is able to establish whether or not it was the weapon used in a crime. Experts are particularly adept in the microscopic examination of spent bullets and cartridge cases. They have access to a world-famous reference collection and computer-based information systems relating to thousands of firearms.

Training

The Service offers training to overseas scientists; this is of a general nature or is aimed at specific techniques, such as DNA profiling or examination of firearms and documents. Training is provided on note-taking, searching, report writing and expert witness appearances in court. Consultancy services are available to other countries on the setting up of new forensic science laboratories.

Research

There is a research and support establishment which ensures that the latest and most effective techniques and equipment are employed by the operational scientist. Contact is maintained with other institutions and universities in Britain and other countries.

The Security Service

The functions of the Security Service are to protect national security, in particular against threats from:

—espionage, terrorism and sabotage;

—the activities of agents of foreign powers; and

—actions intended to overthrow or undermine parliamentary democracy by political, industrial or violent means.

It also exists to safeguard the economic well-being of Britain against external threats.

Under the provisions of legislation passed in 1989, the operations of the Service are under the control of a Director-General appointed by, and accountable to, the Home Secretary. The legislation also established the post of Security Service Commissioner, and the Security Service Tribunal comprising senior members of the legal profession. The Commissioner, appointed by the Prime Minister, keeps under review the issue of property warrants, and assists the Security Service Tribunal, which considers complaints from members of the public who believe the Security Service has done something to them or their property. Complaints about property warrants are considered by the Commissioner.

Any entry on, or interference with, property by the Security Service must be authorised by a warrant issued by the Secretary of State—usually the Home Secretary or Northern Ireland Secretary.

Police Discipline

The police are not above the law and must act within it. A police officer is an agent of the law of the land and may be sued or prosecuted for any wrongful act committed in the performance of police duties. Officers are also subject to a disciplinary code designed to deal with abuse of police powers and maintain public confidence in police impartiality. If found guilty of breaching the code, an officer can be dismissed from the force.

Revised disciplinary procedures for the police in Great Britain, similar to those in operation elsewhere in the public service, are being introduced. These provide for a more flexible system with greater line management involvement, the introduction of unsatisfactory performance procedures and changes in the appeals procedures, which no longer involve the Home Secretary.

England and Wales

Members of the public have the right to make complaints against police officers if they feel that they have been treated unfairly or improperly. In England and Wales the investigation and resolution of complaints is scrutinised by the independent Police Complaints Authority. The Authority must supervise any case involving death or serious injury and has discretion to supervise in any other case. In addition, the Authority reviews chief constables' proposals on whether disciplinary charges should be brought against an officer who has been the subject of a complaint. If the chief constable does not recommend formal disciplinary charges, the Authority may, if it disagrees with the decision, recommend and, if necessary, direct that charges be brought.

Scotland

In Scotland complaints against police officers involving allegations of any form of criminal conduct are referred to the procurator fiscal service (see p. 53) for investigation. The first stage is an initial investigation by senior police officers who report the results to the regional procurator fiscal. If the fiscal is satisfied that an offence has been committed, he or she makes an independent enquiry. Once this is complete, the fiscal can make recommendations to the Crown Office. The Lord Advocate or the Solicitor General decides whether criminal proceedings should take place against the police officer concerned. The Police and Magistrates' Courts Act 1994 empowers the Scottish Inspectorate of Constabulary to consider representations from complainants dissatisfied with the way the police have handled their complaints.

Northern Ireland

In Northern Ireland the Independent Commission for Police Complaints receives copies of all complaints made by members of the public against police officers. The Commission must supervise the police investigation of all complaints which include an allegation of death or serious injury. At its discretion it may also supervise the investigation of any other complaints against an officer. At the end of any supervised investigation the Commission must tell the chief constable whether it is satisfied with the way the investigation was carried out.

There is also a second stage to the complaints procedure in Northern Ireland. Every investigated case, whether supervised by the Commission or not, is referred to it for independent consideration of any possible breaches of discipline. If it considers that a breach of discipline has taken place, it has the power to recommend or order that a disciplinary charge should be brought against the officer. Charges are heard by a tribunal consisting of the chief constable and two members of the Commission who have not previously been concerned with the case; officers who appear before a tribunal can be legally represented. If the Commission considers that a police officer ought to be charged with a criminal offence, it has the power to direct the chief constable to refer the case to the Director of Public Prosecutions.

The Northern Ireland Police Authority can invite the Commission to supervise the investigation of any matter which appears to indicate that a police officer may have committed a criminal or disciplinary offence.

Community Relations

The Government aims to ensure that the quality of service provided by police forces in Britain inspires public confidence, and that the police have the active support and involvement of the communities which they serve.

The police service is taking effective action to improve performance and standards. All forces in England and Wales have to consult with the communities they serve and develop policing policies to meet community demands. In keeping with the Government's Citizen's Charter, the police are required to be more open and explicit about their operations and the standards of service that they offer.

In Scotland the Government's Justice Charter states that chief constables' annual reports should indicate what the force has done to obtain the views of the public on the quality of service provided and the action taken in response to public opinion.

Virtually all forces have liaison departments designed to develop closer contact between the force and the community. Police/community liaison consultative groups operate in every police authority; they consist of representatives from the police, local councillors and community groups.

Particular efforts are made to develop relations with young people through greater contact with schools and their pupils. School governing bodies and head teachers are under an obligation to describe in their annual reports the steps they take to strengthen their schools' links with the community, including the police.

Ethnic Minorities

The Government has repeatedly stated its commitment to improve relations between the police and ethnic minorities. Central guidance recommends that all police officers should receive a thorough training in community and race relations issues. A specialist support unit provides training for police trainers.

The police response to racially motivated incidents is seen by ethnic minority communities as a powerful indicator of the service's commitment to fair treatment for all. Home Office and police initiatives are designed to tackle racially motivated crime and to ensure that the issue is seen as a priority by the police. In addition, forces' responses to racial incidents are monitored by the Inspectorate of Constabulary. Discriminatory behaviour by police officers, either to other officers or to members of the public, is an offence under the Police Discipline Code.

Equal Opportunities

All police forces recognise the need to recruit women and members of the ethnic minorities in order to ensure that the police represent the community. At the end of 1993 there were some 1,730 ethnic minority officers and some 16,750 women police officers in England and Wales. Scottish police forces had 1,680 women officers. Every force has an equal opportunities policy.

Police Training

England and Wales

In England and Wales entry to the police force is open to men and women over the age of 18 and a half. Candidates must be either British or Commonwealth citizens, physically fit and have good eyesight. There are no longer any minimum height requirements. There is an educational test taken by all candidates regardless of educational achievement.

All police officers go through a basic training course lasting several months and spend a total of two years as probationers. Training for probationer constables is a combination of on-the-job training and work at residential training centres.

After the initial two years as probationers, they can apply for promotion to sergeant provided they have passed the qualifying examination. Similarly, if officers have passed the inspector's examination, they can apply for promotion to that rank after two years' service as a sergeant. In order to make sure that officers selected for higher command have the best training, the Home Office has a Police Staff College at Bramshill which trains senior officers. In addition, there is an accelerated promotion scheme for graduate entrants designed to identify officers of the highest calibre for top ranks in the service; all entrants do the basic two years' training and have to sit the same examinations as any other serving officer. However, they are expected to move through the system much faster via the accelerated promotion course at Bramshill. The accelerated promotion course is also available for non-graduate officers with strong potential for rapid promotion to senior ranks.

Regionally run courses are available for all newly promoted sergeants and inspectors, and the Police Staff College also offers a police management programme for all staff in middle management roles. Senior officers also go to the College for a variety of training courses; these include courses for officers assessed as having the potential for chief officer rank. In addition, forces provide a wide range of specialist and general training courses for officers at all stages of their careers.

The Metropolitan Police Force has its own training centre at Hendon in north-west London.

Many forces have developed distance learning packages through the use of videos and closed-circuit television, the aim being to deliver training with minimum time away from operational duties.

Scotland and Northern Ireland

The Scottish Police College provides training for junior and senior officers and for detectives and traffic officers. There are senior command courses as well as an accelerated promotion programme. In addition, in-force training emphasises the practical application of the law in relation to officers' duties.

In Northern Ireland all regular recruits have 14 weeks' initial training, following which they complete a two-year probationary period before their appointments are confirmed.

Policing

The heart of policing is the work done by police constables, who are in constant contact with the public. They patrol the streets on foot, sometimes on bicycles or in cars, give advice and deal with disturbances. They also work at the local police station, handling enquiries and dealing with arrested people. Some specialise, for example, as dog handlers or mounted police. Every force has its criminal investigation department staffed by specialist detectives. There is also a traffic division which operates road patrol units charged with enforcing traffic law and helping motorists in difficulties.

At the heart of most police stations is the control room equipped with high-tech computer and radio equipment. The control room monitors and co-ordinates most of the day-to-day work of the police officer on the beat and provides operational back-up. The central communications room keeps the police officer in touch with other officers and with the station by a personal or car radio. Information from the police computer network is also relayed.

London's Metropolitan Police Force has a central command complex responsible for providing support to areas and divisions during the initial stages of any major incident or public disorder. Incidents involving the use of firearms and high-speed vehicle pursuits also require the co-ordination provided by the central command complex. One part of the complex is responsible for the day-to-day control of traffic within the Metropolitan Police District; it has access to computer systems which monitor traffic flow and control automatic traffic signals at many road junctions.

Firearms

Police officers in England, Scotland and Wales do not normally carry firearms. Uniformed officers may carry wooden truncheons or side-handled, expandable and straight batons to help protect themselves against violence. Firearms may be issued only to specially trained police officers, known as Authorised Firearms Officers, and then only on the authority of a senior officer. Authority is given when an officer is likely to face an armed criminal or is deployed to protect a person who may be at risk of attack. Officers may fire weapons only as a last resort if they believe that their own or other lives are in danger. Each Authorised Firearms Officer is personally responsible for the decision to fire and may be required to justify this action before the courts.

Most forces in England and Wales operate a system of armed response vehicles to provide a speedy initial response to firearms incidents. Officers in armoured response vehicles in London can wear their sidearms in holsters at all times. Elsewhere, this is for the chief officer to decide.

Members of the Royal Ulster Constabulary, in the light of terrorist violence between 1969 and 1994, carry firearms for personal protection.

Civilians

All police forces employ civilians to back up their service to the public. They perform mainly administrative tasks although some civilian work covers scene-of-crime officers who carry out forensic and fingerprint examinations; other civilians take on the jobs of traffic wardens and school-crossing patrols. Civilians become involved whenever a job does not require the special training, experience and powers of police officers, thereby releasing thousands of the latter to concentrate on police duties.

Police Powers

England and Wales

The powers of a police officer in England and Wales to stop and search, arrest and place a person under detention are contained in the Police and Criminal Evidence Act 1984. The legislation and its accompanying codes of practice set out the powers and responsibilities of officers in the investigation of offences, and the rights of citizens.

An officer is liable to disciplinary proceedings if he or she fails to comply with any provision of the codes, and evidence obtained in breach of the codes may be ruled inadmissible in court. The codes must be readily available in all police stations for consultation by police officers, detained people and members of the public.

Stop and Search

A police officer in England and Wales has the power to stop and search people and vehicles if there are reasonable grounds for suspecting that he or she will find stolen goods, offensive weapons or implements that could be used for theft, burglary and other offences. The officer must, however, state and record the grounds for taking this action and what, if anything, was found.

The Criminal Justice and Public Order Act 1994 enables a senior police officer to authorise uniformed officers to stop and search people or vehicles for offensive weapons or dangerous implements where he or she has reasonable grounds for believing that serious incidents of violence may take place. The officer must specify the time scale and area in which the powers are to be exercised.

Arrest

In England and Wales the police have wide powers to arrest people suspected of having committed an offence with or without a warrant issued by a court. For serious offences, known as 'arrestable offences', a suspect can be arrested without a warrant. Arrestable offences are those for which five or more years' imprisonment can be imposed. This category also includes 'serious arrestable offences', such as murder, rape and kidnapping.

There is also a general arrest power for all other offences if it is impracticable or inappropriate to proceed by way of summons to appear in court, or if the police officer has reasonable grounds for believing that arrest is necessary to prevent the person concerned from causing injury to any other person or damage to property.

Detention, Treatment and Questioning

An arrested person must be taken to a police station (if he or she is not already at one) as soon as practicable after arrest. At the station, he or she will be seen by the custody officer, who will consider the reasons for the arrest and whether there are sufficient grounds for the person to be detained. The suspect has a right to speak to an independent solicitor free of charge and to have a relative or other named person told of his or her arrest. Where a person has been arrested in connection with a serious arrestable offence, but has not yet been charged, the police may delay the exercise of these rights for up to 36 hours in the interests of the investigation if certain strict criteria are met.

A suspect may refuse to answer police questions or to give evidence in court. Changes to this so-called 'right to silence' have been made by the Criminal Justice and Public Order Act 1994 to allow courts in England and Wales to draw inferences from a defendant's refusal to answer police questions or to give information during his or her trial. Reflecting this change in the law, a new form of police caution (which must precede any questions to a suspect for the purpose of obtaining evidence) is intended to ensure that people understand the possible consequences if they answer questions or stay silent.

Questions relating to an offence may not normally be put to a person after he or she has been charged with that offence or informed that he or she may be prosecuted for it.

The length of time a suspect is held in police custody before charge is strictly regulated. For lesser offences this may not exceed 24 hours. A person suspected of committing a serious arrestable offence can be detained for up to 96 hours without charge but beyond 36 hours only if a warrant is obtained from a magistrates' court. Reviews must be made of a person's detention at regular intervals—six hours after initial detention and thereafter every nine hours as a maximum—to check whether the criteria for detention are still satisfied. If they are not, the person must be released immediately.

The tape recording of interviews with suspected offenders at police stations must be used when the police are investigating indictable offences and in certain other cases. The police are not precluded from taping interviews for other types of offence. The taping of interviews is regulated by a code of practice approved by Parliament, and the suspect is entitled to a copy of the tape.

People detained in custody who think that the grounds for their detention are unlawful may apply to the High Court in England and Wales for a writ of *habeas corpus* (a writ requiring a person to be brought before a court to investigate the lawfulness of his or her restraint) against the person who detained them. The person responsible must appear in court on a day named to justify the detention. *Habeas corpus* proceedings take precedence over others.

Recognising that the use of DNA analysis has become a powerful tool in the investigation of crime, the Government has extended police powers to take body samples from suspects. The Criminal Justice and Public Order Act 1994 allows the police to take non-intimate samples without consent from anyone who is detained or convicted for a recordable offence, and to use the samples to search against existing records of convicted offenders or unsolved crimes. In time a national database will be built up.

Charging

Once there is sufficient evidence, the police have to decide whether a detained person should be charged with the offence. If there is insufficient evidence to charge, the person may be released on bail pending further enquiries by the police. The police may decide to take no further action in respect of a particular offence and to release the person. Alternatively, they may decide to issue him or her with a formal caution (see p. 69), which will be recorded and may be taken into account if he or she subsequently re-offends.

If charged with an offence, a person may be kept in custody if there is a risk that he or she might fail to appear in court or might interfere with the administration of justice. When no such considerations apply, the person must be released on or without bail. Where someone is detained after charge, he or she must be brought before a magistrates' court as soon as practicable. This is usually no later than the next working day.

Scotland

The police in Scotland can arrest a person without a warrant if he or she is seen committing a crime. This also applies to a person reasonably suspected of an offence against laws controlling the use of drugs. In other cases the police may seek a warrant to arrest a person suspected of a crime by applying to a justice naming the person, the crime and the reason for the warrant. Once the warrant is granted, the police can arrest the suspect.

Scottish police have powers to enter a building without a warrant from a court if they are in close pursuit of a person who has committed or attempted to commit a serious crime. A court can grant the police a search warrant empowering them to search premises for stated items in connection with a crime. The police have statutory powers to search any person if they have reasonable grounds to suspect him or her of carrying an offensive weapon.

There are powers to detain for questioning anyone the police suspect of committing an offence punishable by imprisonment. The suspect may not be detained for more than six hours. After this period the person must be either formally arrested and charged or released. If held in a police station, the suspect has a right to have a solicitor and one other person informed about his or her whereabouts.

Once a person has been charged with a criminal offence, only voluntary statements will normally be allowed in evidence at the trial. The court will reject statements unless satisfied that they have been fairly obtained. Tape recording of interviews with suspects is common practice. Anyone arrested must be brought before a court on the first working day after arrest. In less serious cases, the police may release a person who gives a written undertaking to attend court at a later date.

Where the charges involve serious crime, the accused is brought before the sheriff in private, either to be committed for a period not exceeding eight days to allow further enquiries to be made or to be committed for trial.

The Criminal Justice (Scotland) Act 1995 provides for an extension of the range of samples which the police in Scotland may take without warrant for DNA analysis.

Northern Ireland

Non-emergency police powers in Northern Ireland are the same as in England and Wales. Tape recording of interviews is being extended to cover all police stations.

Under emergency legislation designed to combat terrorism, people detained on suspicion of terrorist offences are kept at special holding centres, and may be held for up to 48 hours. Further extensions of up to five days require the consent of the Secretary of State.

Awaiting Trial

England and Wales

There are time limits on the period a defendant may be remanded in custody awaiting trial in England and Wales. In cases tried before a magistrates' court these are generally 56 days from first appearance to trial or 70 days between first appearance to referral to trial in the Crown Court. The limit in Crown Court cases is 112 days from referral from the magistrates' court to taking of the plea. There are some cases where it is not possible to comply with the time limit, and the courts have powers to extend limits if satisfied that there is a good reason and the prosecution has acted as quickly as possible.

Most accused people are released on bail pending trial. They are not remanded in custody except where strictly necessary. In England and Wales the court decides whether a defendant should be released on bail. Unconditional bail may be withheld only if the court has substantial grounds for believing that the accused would abscond, commit an offence, interfere with witnesses, or otherwise obstruct the course of justice.

A court may also impose conditions before granting bail. If bail is refused, the defendant may apply to a High Court judge or to the Crown Court for bail. In certain circumstances, the prosecution may appeal to a Crown Court judge against the granting of bail by magistrates. An application can also be made to the Crown Court for conditions imposed by a magistrates' court to be altered.

In some cases a court may grant bail to a defendant on condition that he or she lives in an approved bail or probation/bail hostel.

The probation service's bail information schemes provide the Crown Prosecution Service with verified information about a defendant. This assists the Service to decide whether to oppose bail and enables the courts to take an informed decision on whether to grant bail.

The Criminal Justice and Public Order Act 1994 gives the police powers of immediate arrest for breach of police bail and removes the presumption in favour of bail for people alleged to have offended while on bail. It also restricts the right to bail for someone charged with murder, manslaughter or rape if previously convicted of the same offence.

Scotland

When arrested, an accused person in Scotland may be released by the police to await summons, on an undertaking to appear at court at a specified time, or be held in custody to appear at court on the next lawful day. Following that appearance, the accused may be remanded in custody until trial or released by the court on bail. If released on bail, the accused must undertake to appear at trial when required, not to commit an offence while on bail, and not to interfere with witnesses or obstruct the course of justice. The court may also impose additional conditions on the accused as appropriate (for example, to keep away from certain people or locations).

There is a right of appeal to the High Court by an accused person against the refusal of bail, or by the prosecutor against the granting of bail, or by either against the conditions imposed.

The Criminal Justice (Scotland) Act 1995 gives the courts increased powers to sentence a person who commits an offence while on bail. A prison sentence may be increased by up to six months; a fine by up to £1,000. Bail will not be granted where an accused person is charged with murder, attempted murder, culpable homicide, rape or attempted rape and has a previous conviction for such a crime (in the case of culpable homicide involving a prison sentence).

If a person charged with a serious offence has been kept in custody pending trial, the trial must begin within 110 days of the date of full committal. The trial of a person released on bail on a serious offence must begin within 12 months of the first appearance in court on that charge. The trial of a person charged with a summary offence and held in custody must begin within 40 days of the date of first appearance in court.

Northern Ireland

In Northern Ireland bail may be granted by a resident magistrate except in cases dealt with under emergency provisions (see p. 12), where the decision is made by a judge of the High Court.

Criminal Courts

England and Wales

Prosecution

The Crown Prosecution Service (CPS) is responsible for the prosecution of almost all criminal cases resulting from police investigations. A government department which is independent in its decision-taking, the CPS is headed by the Director of Public Prosecutions, who is accountable to Parliament through the Attorney General (see p. 89) . It is divided into 13 areas, each of which is headed by a Chief Crown Prosecutor.

The CPS became operational in 1986 and was created in order to separate the investigation of crime from its prosecution. Previously the police had been responsible for prosecutions.

The CPS reviews evidence collected by the police in relation to a particular offence and decides whether a prosecution should be brought. Decisions are reached by applying two criteria—the evidential test and the public interest test—which are set out in the Code for Crown Prosecutors. Crown Prosecutors must be satisfied that there is enough evidence to provide 'a realistic prospect of conviction' against each defendant on each charge, and that the evidence can be used and is reliable. Having satisfied himself or herself that the evidence can justify proceedings, the Crown Prosecutor must then consider whether the public interest requires a prosecution. Only cases which meet both these criteria should be prosecuted.

In nearly all cases the decision to prosecute is delegated to lawyers in the area offices. However, some especially sensitive or complex cases, including terrorist offences and breaches of the Official Secrets Act, are dealt with by the CPS headquarters in London.

The Serious Fraud Office (SFO) prosecutes the most serious and complex cases of fraud in England, Wales and Northern Ireland. Investigations are conducted by teams of lawyers, accountants, police officers and other specialists. A review of the relative responsibilities of the SFO and the CPS's Fraud Divisions has concluded that the existing separate structures should be retained.

Courts

Very serious offences, such as murder, manslaughter, rape and robbery are tried upon indictment' (or formal accusation) only by the Crown Court, where all contested trials are presided over by a judge sitting with a jury (see p. 46). Summary offences—the least serious offences and the vast majority of criminal cases—are tried by unpaid lay magistrates or by a few paid stipendiary magistrates; both sit without a jury.

A third category of offences—such as theft, the less serious cases of burglary and some assaults—are known as 'either way' offences. They can be tried either by magistrates' courts or by jury in the Crown Court. If magistrates are content to deal with the case, the accused has the right to choose trial by magistrates or trial by jury in the Crown Court.

The cases of all those charged with offences triable in the Crown Court must first be considered by a magistrates' court, which decides whether to send them to the Court for trial. As recommended by the Royal Commission, a new administrative procedure for transferring cases to the Crown Court is replacing all committal proceedings under the provisions of the Criminal Justice and Public Order Act 1994. The defence can still argue that there is no case to answer and the magistrates' courts have a discretion to admit, on application, oral argument by the defence. No witnesses are called to give evidence. Existing procedures for transferring cases of serious or complex fraud (see p. 47) or cases involving child evidence (see p. 48) are not affected by the legislation.

Magistrates' Courts

A magistrates' court, which is open to the public and the media, usually consists of three lay magistrates—known as justices of the peace—who are advised by a justices' clerk or an assistant. The justices' clerk must be a qualified lawyer. In addition to advising the bench on law and procedure, he or she manages the court and court offices. Justices' clerks and other staff are appointed by local magistrates' courts committees, which are elected by magistrates in the area.

There are about 30,000 lay magistrates, who must be trained in court procedures and aware of the rules of evidence. They are recommended for the job by committees of local people; when new magistrates are needed, the committees seek nominations from local organisations or businesses. The local committee is expected to make sure that magistrates are drawn from many walks of life and that the composition of the bench is broadly balanced. Most are appointed by the Lord Chancellor and the remainder by the Chancellor of the Duchy of Lancaster. The Police and Magistrates' Courts Act 1994 is designed to improve the local accountability of magistrates' courts committees, giving them the power to combine or otherwise adjust their areas.

The few full-time, legally qualified stipendiary magistrates may sit alone and usually preside in courts in urban areas where the workload is heavy.

Most cases involving people under 18 are heard in youth courts. These are specialist magistrates' courts which either sit apart from other courts or are held at a different time. Restrictions are placed on access by ordinary members of the public. Media reports must not identify a young person concerned in the proceedings, whether as defendant, victim or witness. (However, a juvenile charged with a serious offence who is unlawfully at large may be identified.)

Where a young person under 18 is charged jointly with someone of 18 or over, the case may be heard in an ordinary magistrates' court or the Crown Court. If the young person is found guilty, the court may transfer the case to a youth court for sentence.

Where a young person is charged with homicide, he or she must be tried in the Crown Court. Juveniles aged 14 or over who are charged with an offence carrying a sentence of 14 years' imprisonment or more may be tried in the Crown Court.

An independent inspectorate monitors the administration and management of magistrates' courts in order to improve performance and spread good practice. It is not empowered to comment on the judicial decisions of magistrates or their clerks in particular cases.

The Crown Court

The Crown Court sits at 93 venues and is presided over by High Court judges, full-time 'circuit judges' and part-time recorders. The kind of judge chosen to preside over the case depends on its seriousness and complexity. Crown Court organisation is based on six regional areas called circuits, each of which has two or more presiding judges who are responsible for judicial administration of the circuit. Circuit judges have delegated judicial responsibilities at large Crown Court centres or for a number of smaller ones.

Courts Charter

A Courts Charter, setting out the standards of service which apply in the higher courts in England and Wales, came into operation in January 1993. It outlines arrangements to help court users and ease the strains associated with court attendance.

A new Charter, called the 'Charter for Court Users', was launched in July 1995. It gives more information about court systems and procedures and has new standards on, for example, the treatment of victims and witnesses and on complaints handling. It does not cover judicial decisions.

Trial Procedure

Criminal trials in England and Wales, as in the rest of Britain, have two parties: the prosecution and the defence. The prosecution must prove beyond reasonable doubt that the defendant committed the crime alleged. The law presumes the innocence of an accused person until guilt has been proven. An accused person has the right to employ a legal adviser and may be granted legal aid from public funds (see p. 93). If remanded in custody, he or she may be visited by a legal adviser to ensure a properly prepared defence.

In Crown Court cases the prosecution must disclose to the defence at an early stage all the statements from the witnesses upon whom it proposes to rely. This duty does not apply to offences tried in the magistrates' court, except when advance information is required by the defence in 'either way' cases (see p. 40). There is also a general duty to disclose to the defence evidence, documents and information which might have a bearing on the defence case. In circumstances where the material attracts public interest immunity (where the public interest in secrecy outweighs the public interest in doing justice to the individual) or is otherwise subject to a duty of confidentiality, the prosecution is obliged to place it before the court for a ruling.

The Government has put forward proposals for a reform of the law on prosecution and defence disclosure in England and Wales. These would:

—reduce the burden on police and prosecution of disclosing large volumes of material to the defence even though much of it may not be relevant to the real issues;

—provide better protection for sensitive material, such as the identity of police informants; and

—require the defence to disclose its main line of argument before the trial so as to narrow the issues in dispute.

Criminal trials are normally held in public—in what is known as 'open court'—and rules of evidence, which are concerned with the proof of facts, are rigorously applied. If evidence is improperly admitted, a conviction can be quashed on appeal. Hearsay evidence is generally not admissible.

The mandatory warning given by judges to juries in trials of sexual offences that it is dangerous to convict the accused solely on the basis of the unsupported evidence of the victim or of an accomplice has been abolished under the Criminal Justice and Public Order Act 1994.

Table 2: Offenders Found Guilty at All Courts in England and Wales By Sex and Type of Offence

Number of Male (M) and Female (F) offenders (thousands)

Type of Offence	1992		1993		1994	
	M	F	M	F	M	F
Indictable offences						
Violence against the person	39.8	3.8	35.5	3.4	33.9	3.7
Sexual offences	4.9	0.1	4.3	0.1	4.4	0.0
Burglary	43.0	1.2	39.2	1.0	37.0	1.0
Robbery	4.8	0.3	4.8	0.3	4.5	0.4
Theft and handling stolen goods	103.9	24.0	99.5	22.1	99.1	22.5
Fraud and forgery	15.6	4.4	13.6	3.9	14.2	4.2
Criminal damage	9.0	0.8	8.6	0.8	9.2	0.8
Drug offences	20.6	2.1	19.9	2.0	25.3	2.5
Other (excluding motoring offences)	33.1	2.9	34.2	3.6	35.5	3.8
Motoring offences	10.3	0.4	10.3	0.5	11.4	0.6
Total	**284.9**	**40.0**	**269.8**	**37.8**	**274.6**	**39.5**
Summary offences						
Offences (excluding motoring offences)	322.5	149.2	307.0	146.1	308.4	146.3
Motoring offences	653.3	69.8	597.5	67.2	573.6	65.2
Total	**975.8**	**219.0**	**904.4**	**213.3**	**882.0**	**211.5**
All offences	**1,260.7**	**259.0**	**1,174.3**	**251.1**	**1,156.6**	**251.0**

Source: *Criminal Statistics England and Wales 1994.*

A defendant cannot be questioned without consenting to be sworn as a witness in his or her own defence, although a court may, under recent legislation, draw inferences from a refusal to give evidence. If he or she does testify, cross-examination about character or other conduct may be made only in exceptional circumstances. Generally, the prosecution may not introduce such evidence.

In a magistrates' court the trial begins when the justices' clerk reads out details of the offence with which the defendant is charged. In Crown Court jury trials it starts with the reading of a formal document called the indictment, setting out the accusation made against the defendant.

In both types of trial the prosecution then presents its case, backed up by its witnesses. The defendant can address the court in person or through a lawyer, who cross-examines the prosecution witnesses and presents the defence case. The prosecuting lawyer can cross-examine defence witnesses. Once the witnesses have given their evidence, the prosecuting lawyer makes a closing speech, followed by that of the defence lawyer, who has the right to the last speech at the trial.

In magistrates' court proceedings the bench of three magistrates takes the decision on whether the defendant is guilty or not guilty.

The Jury

In Crown Court jury trials the judge decides questions of law, sums up the evidence for the jury after prosecution and defence closing speeches, and discharges the accused or passes sentence. The jury is responsible for deciding whether a defendant is 'guilty' or 'not guilty', the latter verdict resulting in acquittal. If the jury cannot reach a unanimous verdict, the judge may permit it to bring in a majority verdict provided that, in the normal jury of 12 people, there are not more than two dissenters.

If the jury acquits the defendant, the prosecution has no right of appeal and the defendant cannot be tried again for the same offence. The defendant, however, has a right of appeal to a higher court if found guilty (see p. 50).

A jury is independent of the judiciary. Any attempt to interfere with a jury is a criminal offence. Potential jurors are put on a panel before the start of the trial. The prosecution and the defence may challenge individual jurors on the panel, giving reasons for doing so.

People between the ages of 18 and 70 whose names appear on the electoral register, with certain exceptions, are liable for jury service and their names are chosen at random. Ineligible people include, for example, judges and people who within the previous ten years have been members of the legal profession or the police, prison or probation services. People convicted of certain offences within the previous ten years cannot serve on a jury. Anyone who has received a prison sentence of five years or more is disqualified for life. Under the Criminal Justice and Public Order Act 1994, people on bail are also ineligible to sit on juries.

Fraud Cases

In complex fraud cases the judge may order a preparatory Crown Court hearing to be held. It is in open court but subject to restrictions on press reporting. This provides an opportunity for the judge to determine questions regarding admissibility of evidence and any other questions of law relating to the case. The judge also has the power to order the prosecution and the defence to serve on each other certain statements and to prepare the case in such a way that it is easier to understand. Appeals may be made to the Court of Appeal from certain decisions of the judge in the preparatory hearings.

Legislation in 1987 provided for the by-passing of the magistrates' court in cases of serious and complex fraud. In such cases, designated authorities, such as the Director of the Serious

Fraud Office, may give notice of transfer in order to bring proceedings before the Crown Court.

Child Witnesses

The Criminal Justice Act 1988 abolished the presumption that children were incompetent as witnesses. It also introduced the system which allows children to give their evidence at court by means of a closed-circuit television link. Building on that, the Criminal Justice Act 1991 extended the closed-circuit television provisions, forbade the cross-examination of a child directly by the accused, and provided for a video-recorded interview with a child victim or witness to be admissible in court as his or her main evidence.

The Act also provided for committal proceedings in magistrates' courts to be by-passed in cases involving child evidence. In such cases, however, the defence could apply to the Crown Court judge if it believed that there was insufficient evidence to proceed.

The Criminal Justice and Public Order Act 1994 further clarified the law on child evidence, by requiring judges to admit the evidence of a child unless he or she is incapable of giving intelligible testimony. It is for the jury to decide what weight should be placed on a child's evidence.

Sentencing

If a person is convicted, the magistrate or judge decides on the most appropriate sentence. Account is taken of the facts of the offence, the circumstances of the offender, any previous convictions and sentences and any statutory limits on sentencing. The defence lawyer may make a speech in mitigation.

Flow Chart of the Criminal Justice System in England and Wales, 1994

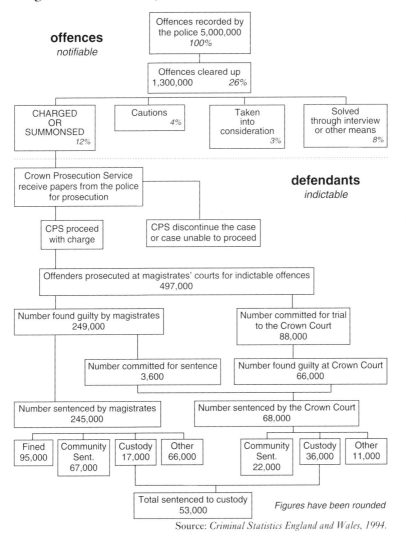

offences
notifiable

Offences recorded by
the police 5,000,000
100%

Offences cleared up
1,300,000   *26%*

| CHARGED OR SUMMONSED *12%* | Cautions *4%* | Taken into consideration *3%* | Solved through interview or other means *8%* |

Crown Prosecution Service
receive papers from the police
for prosecution

defendants
indictable

CPS proceed
with charge

CPS discontinue the case
or case unable to proceed

Offenders prosecuted at magistrates' courts for indictable offences
497,000

Number found guilty by magistrates
249,000

Number committed for trial
to the Crown Court
88,000

Number committed for sentence
3,600

Number found guilty at Crown Court
66,000

Number sentenced by magistrates
245,000

Number sentenced by the Crown Court
68,000

| Fined 95,000 | Community Sent. 67,000 | Custody 17,000 | Other 66,000 | Community Sent. 22,000 | Custody 36,000 | Other 11,000 |

Total sentenced to custody
53,000

Figures have been rounded

Source: *Criminal Statistics England and Wales, 1994.*

The Criminal Justice Act 1991 places a requirement on the courts in England and Wales to obtain a 'pre-sentence' report from the probation service on offenders under the age of 18 in cases involving an offence triable either way before passing a custodial or more complex community sentence. In most other circumstances, such reports are discretionary. Revised national standards for the supervision of offenders in the community in 1995 require that pre-sentence reports include a new section in which the impact of the offence on the victim is explained to the court.

The Criminal Justice and Public Order Act 1994 provides for sentence discounts for those pleading guilty at an early stage in the court process, giving effect to a recommendation of the Royal Commission on Criminal Justice.

Appeals

A person convicted by a magistrates' court may appeal to the Crown Court against the sentence imposed if he or she has pleaded guilty. An appeal may be made against both conviction and sentence, or sentence alone, if a 'not guilty' plea has been made. The Divisional Court of the Queen's Bench Division of the High Court hears appeals on points of law and procedure—by either prosecution or defence—in cases originally dealt with by magistrates.

If convicted by the Crown Court, a defendant may seek leave to appeal to the Court of Appeal (Criminal Division) against both the conviction and the sentence imposed. The Court is presided over by the Lord Chief Justice. Lawyers in the Criminal Appeal Office examine applications for leave to appeal, and a judge decides whether the case should be allowed to proceed to the full Court of Appeal. If leave to appeal is granted or the case referred to the full Court, the lawyer writes a summary for the Court setting out the facts of the case and drawing the attention of the Court to any relevant points of law or cases which may be of assistance. The more difficult or complex cases are dealt with by a small team of special case lawyers.

The House of Lords is the final appeal court, but it will consider only those cases that involve a point of law of general public importance and where leave to appeal is granted.

The Attorney General may seek a ruling of the Court of Appeal on a point of law which has been material in a case where a person is tried on indictment. The Court has power to refer the point to the House of Lords if necessary. The ruling will constitute a binding precedent, but an acquittal in the original case is not affected.

The Attorney General has the power to apply for leave to refer to the Court of Appeal for reconsideration a sentence imposed in the Crown Court if it is, in his or her view, unduly lenient. Originally, only a sentence imposed in respect of offences triable only on indictment could be reviewed. However, the Attorney General's power has been extended. Although any sentence for consideration must still have been passed by the Crown Court, certain triable 'either way' offences are now covered. These are indecent assault, making threats to kill, and cruelty to, or neglect of, a child. The Attorney General's power has been further extended to cover certain types of serious or complex fraud. The Court of Appeal may, if it is minded to quash the original sentence, impose in its place any sentence which the original sentencing court had the power to impose.

Criminal Cases Review Commission

On the basis of recommendations of the Royal Commission on Criminal Justice and subsequent consultations, new legislation has been passed on criminal appeals. The Criminal Appeal Act 1995 provides for the creation of a Criminal Cases Review Commission to operate in England, Wales and Northern Ireland. This body, independent of both Government and the courts, will examine possible miscarriages of justice in cases tried on indictment or summarily and decide whether to refer them to the courts on the grounds of sentence and conviction. It will direct and supervise investigations undertaken on its behalf and approve the appointment of investigating officers. Referral of a case will require some new argument or evidence not previously raised at the trial or on appeal.

The final decision on any case referred will rest with the respective Courts of Appeal in England and Wales and Northern Ireland (if the case was tried originally on indictment) or with the Crown Court following a referral in a summary case. The courts will therefore continue to be responsible for determining all appeals whether made to them direct or on referral by the Commission.

The power of the Home Secretary (and the Secretary of State in Northern Ireland) to investigate and refer cases to the Court of Appeal where a miscarriage of justice may have occurred will be relinquished. The legislation also clarifies the grounds for allowing and dismissing an appeal—the Court of Appeal will allow any appeal where it considers the conviction unsafe and will dismiss it in any other case.

The Home Secretary will retain the power to recommend the exercise of the Royal Prerogative of Mercy in exceptional cases which could not be dealt with through the appeal process.

Scotland

Prosecution

The prosecution of crime in the Scottish courts is a public function. The police report details of alleged crimes to prosecutors, who decide whether or not to prosecute. Proceedings are initiated by the Lord Advocate with the assistance of:

—the Solicitor General for Scotland;

—Advocates Depute, who are practising lawyers; and

—regional procurators fiscal, who are appointed by the Lord Advocate as his local representatives in each sheriff court district.

Prosecutions in the High Court of Justiciary (see p. 55) are conducted by the Lord Advocate, by the Solicitor General for Scotland (the Lord Advocate's ministerial deputy) or one of the 12 Advocates Depute, who are collectively known as Crown Counsel. In all other criminal courts the prosecutor is the regional procurator fiscal or, more likely, one of his deputes, all of whom are legally qualified. The Lord Advocate is the head of the Crown Office, a civil service department through which he discharges his responsibility for criminal prosecution.

The permanent adviser to the Lord Advocate on prosecution matters is the Crown Agent, who is head of the Procurator Fiscal Service and is assisted by the Crown Office and its legally qualified civil servants.

Initial investigations of crime are made by the police, although the procurator fiscal has the power, and in some cases the duty, to take personal control of an investigation.

Once a police report has been made to the fiscal, he or she decides whether or not to start criminal proceedings. There is no rule of law stating that every criminal offence must be prosecuted. A prosecution is instituted only when the public interest requires it. When taking the decision on prosecution, the fiscal must consider whether:

—a crime has been committed;

—the evidence is sufficient, admissible and reliable; and

—the subject matter is serious enough to warrant a prosecution in the public interest.

When dealing with minor crime, for instance, the fiscal makes use of various alternatives to prosecution, such as formal warnings or diversion to social work. The Criminal Justice (Scotland) Act 1995 provides for an extension of fiscal fines to a wider range of minor offences.

The fiscal can also refer a suitable case for reparation and mediation to an agency; provided both the accused and the victim agree, an arrangement is made between them which will meet the circumstances of the case. This may involve the payment of money by the accused in order to compensate the victim.

Where an accusation of a more serious offence is to be made, the fiscal brings the accused before the sheriff to be committed for further examination or trial. At this stage the accused may be detained in custody pending trial or released on bail. The fiscal may examine the accused before the sheriff; at such proceedings the accused has the opportunity to put forward a special defence, such as alibi, or make a statement about the circumstances of any confession allegedly made.

The Criminal Justice (Scotland) Act 1995 strengthens the procedures for judicial examination of the accused before trial and introduces an enhanced system of intermediate diets (sittings of the sheriff and district courts in advance of the trial) to establish the state of readiness of both the defence and the prosecution. The procedures should reduce inconvenience to both police and civilian witnesses, and should ensure that less time is wasted on trips to court that are not needed.

When preparing the prosecution case, the fiscal must be satisfied that there is evidence to prove the charge beyond reasonable doubt. After the case is prepared, the fiscal sends the papers to the Crown Office for legal examination. If Crown lawyers are satisfied that the evidence is sufficient to justify proceedings, instructions are issued to the fiscal to proceed with the prosecution. Crown lawyers can also order prosecution to take place in the High Court of Justiciary for very serious crimes.

Fraud Cases

The Crown Office Fraud Unit investigates and prepares—in co-operation with the police and other agencies—prosecutions against fraud. In some cases, lawyers in the Unit are nominated by the Lord Advocate to exercise powers equivalent to those of the Serious Fraud Office in England and Wales. The Unit also deals with drug profit confiscation procedures and international criminal investigations and procedures.

Courts

The supreme criminal court in Scotland is the High Court of Justiciary, which consists of the Lord Justice General, the Lord Justice Clerk and other judges. The High Court sits in Edinburgh and in other major towns and cities. It tries the most serious crimes and has exclusive jurisdiction in cases involving murder, treason and rape.

The sheriff court is concerned with relatively less serious offences. There are six sheriffdoms, each of which is headed by a sheriff principal who is responsible for ensuring the efficient disposal of justice. The six sheriffdoms are subdivided into a total of

49 sheriff court districts. The sheriff is the judge in the sheriff court.

District courts deal with more minor offences. They are established on a local government district basis and their judges are either lay justices of the peace or legally qualified stipendiary magistrates who have the same summary criminal jurisdiction and powers as the sheriff (see below).

The fiscal decides whether the case should be tried in the sheriff or district court and whether the proceedings are to be by summary or solemn procedure. Summary procedure leads to trial by a judge sitting alone and solemn procedure to trial by a judge and jury. An accused person does not have the right to elect for trial by jury. When deciding between solemn or summary procedure, the fiscal has to consider the gravity of the offence, the criminal record of the accused and the fact that a summary court has limited powers of sentence in the event of conviction.

In solemn procedure the trial takes place before a judge sitting with a jury of 15 people. Details of the alleged offence are set out in an indictment. The judge decides questions of law and the jury questions of fact.

The judge sits without a jury in summary procedure and decides questions of fact and law. The fiscal serves upon the accused a summary complaint containing the terms of the charge or charges and instructing him or her to appear in court.

All cases in the High Court and the more serious ones in sheriff courts are tried by a judge and jury. Summary procedure is used in the less serious cases in the sheriff courts and in all cases in the district courts.

Children under 16 who have committed an offence are normally dealt with by children's hearings (see p. 86).

Trial Procedure

In solemn procedure the prosecution must give to the defence advance notice of the witnesses it intends to call and of the documents and other items on which it will rely. Rules of evidence similar to those in England and Wales apply in the Scottish courts. The accused person must plead 'guilty' or 'not guilty'. If the accused pleads guilty, the fiscal narrates the facts of the case to the court and provides information to the court about any previous convictions. The judge then disposes of the case.

In contested cases the fiscal questions the prosecution witnesses, and the defence lawyer cross-examines them. This process is reversed when the accused and the defence witnesses give their evidence. Once these procedures have been concluded, the fiscal and the defence lawyer address the court, the defence traditionally having the last word. In summary procedure the judge then decides guilt or acquittal. In jury trials the judge gives appropriate directions in law (the judge's charge) to the jurors before they retire to reach their verdict.

The jury's verdict may be 'guilty', 'not guilty' or 'not proven'; the accused is acquitted if either of the last two verdicts is given. A verdict of 'guilty' can be reached only if at least eight members of the jury are in favour. As a general rule no one may be convicted unless all the essential elements of the charge are proved by corroborated evidence from at least two independent sources. This rule is a safeguard against miscarriages of justice.

The jury consists of 15 jurors, and selection is on a similar basis to that in England and Wales, the same qualifications applying. The upper age limit on Scottish jurors is 65.

If found guilty in a jury trial, the accused is sentenced by the judge in the High Court and by the sheriff in the sheriff court.

Under summary procedure, sentencing is the responsibility of the sheriff in the sheriff court or the lay justices in the district court. It is mandatory for a court to obtain a social enquiry report before imposing a custodial sentence where the accused is under 21 or has not previously served a custodial sentence. A report is also required before making a probation or community service order (see p. 66), or in cases involving people subject to supervision. In other cases the judge decides whether to obtain such a report.

Criminal Justice (Scotland) Act 1995

New legislation provides for improved procedures for the selection of juries, including the abolition of peremptory challenge, and removes the prohibition on the prosecutor to comment on an accused person's failure to give evidence. It also allows the courts to consider hearsay evidence in particular circumstances. In addition, the legislation contains provisions on sentencing:

—courts may take into account the fact that an accused person pleaded guilty, and the timing and circumstances in which the plea was made, when deciding the appropriate sentence; and

—the Appeal Court may issue opinions on the appropriate sentence for cases similar to the particular case before it, and lower courts would be required to have regard to those opinions.

Child Witnesses

Live television links installed in a number of criminal courts enable children to give their evidence without entering the court room. A child's evidence may also be given from behind a screen. Corroboration of the child's evidence is necessary to sustain a conviction.

Appeals

In both solemn and summary procedure an appeal may be brought by the accused against conviction, or sentence, or both. When a case is appealed, the fiscal sends a report to the Crown Office Appeals Unit, which deals centrally with all appeals. The Unit's staff consider the fiscal's report and provide written notes for the Advocates Depute, who usually appear for the Crown in the High Court of Justiciary, sitting as the Court of Criminal Appeal.

The Court may authorise a retrial if it sets aside a conviction, although this rarely occurs. There is no further appeal to the House of Lords. The Crown, too, has certain rights of appeal, although these are used sparingly. It can appeal against acquittal in summary cases where it is considered that the sheriff or justice erred in law in acquitting the accused. This right does not exist for cases prosecuted before a jury, although the Lord Advocate may seek the opinion of the Appeal Court on a point of law which has arisen in a solemn case where an acquittal has resulted; while this procedure does not affect the accused's acquittal, it allows the Appeal Court to clarify the points of law involved. The Crown has a right of appeal against lenient sentences in both solemn and summary procedure.

An accused person may appeal to the Appeal Court on grounds of miscarriage of justice, which may include reference to additional evidence which was not available at the trial.

The Appeals Unit sends out circulars on Appeal Court decisions to all fiscals' offices to ensure that staff are kept informed of such matters. It also maintains close contact with the Lord Advocate's Secretariat, since Appeal Court decisions can have a bearing on proposed changes in legislation or may themselves make legislation necessary.

An independent committee is reviewing whether any changes are needed to the current criteria for the consideration of appeals by the Appeal Court and to the machinery for handling alleged miscarriages of justice. This committee should report in 1996.

The Criminal Justice (Scotland) Act 1995 provides for the introduction of a requirement for leave to appeal. This will involve a single judge assessing whether there are arguable grounds for an appeal. The legislation also reduces the number of High Court judges required to consider appeals against sentence only from three to two.

Northern Ireland

The Director of Public Prosecutions for Northern Ireland prosecutes all offences tried on indictment, and does so in certain summary cases. Most summary offences, however, are prosecuted by the police.

Summary offences are heard in magistrates' courts by a full-time, legally qualified resident magistrate. Offenders under 17 are dealt with by a juvenile court consisting of a legally qualified resident magistrate and two lay members (at least one of whom must be a woman) specially trained to deal with juveniles.

The Crown Court deals with criminal trials on indictment. It is served by High Court and county court judges. Proceedings are heard by a single judge, and all contested cases, other than those involving terrorist-type offences specified under emergency legislation, take place before a jury.

People accused of terrorist-type offences are tried by a judge sitting alone without a jury because of the possibility of jurors being intimidated by terrorist organisations or bringing in perverse verdicts. The onus remains on the prosecution to prove guilt beyond reasonable doubt, and the defendant has the right to be represented by a lawyer of his or her choice. The judge must set out in a written statement the reasons for convicting and there is an automatic right of appeal against conviction and sentence (unless it is one fixed by law) on points of fact as well as of law.

The presentation of evidence in court follows the same pattern as in England and Wales, and jurors are chosen on the same basis. Each defendant, however, has the right to challenge up to 12 potential jurors without giving a reason.

The procedures for dealing with complex fraud cases are the same as those in England and Wales.

Appeals from magistrates' courts against conviction or sentence are heard by the county court. An appeal on a point of law alone can be heard by the Northern Ireland Court of Appeal, which also hears appeals from the Crown Court against conviction and/ or sentence. Procedures for a further appeal to the House of Lords are similar to those in England and Wales.

The Criminal Cases Review Commission (see p. 51) will operate in Northern Ireland as well as in England and Wales.

Treatment of Offenders

The Government believes that prison is the right response for the most serious, dangerous and persistent offenders. It also considers that there should be effective and demanding punishment within the community to deal with offenders for whom a prison sentence is not appropriate. Tough new national standards for community sentences were announced in March 1995. Fines continue to represent a proper penalty for other less serious offences.

Legislation sets the maximum penalties for offences, the sentence being entirely a matter for the courts, subject to these maxima. The Court of Appeal issues guidance to the lower courts on sentencing issues when points of principle have arisen on individual appeal cases.

In Scotland, where many offences are not created by statute, the penalty for offences at common law range from absolute discharge to life imprisonment.

Custody

England and Wales

A custodial sentence is the most severe penalty available to the courts. Under the Criminal Justice Act 1991, a custodial sentence can be imposed only where the offence is so serious that only such a sentence would be appropriate, or where there is a need to protect the public from a sexual or violent offender. A court is required to explain to the offender why it is passing a custodial sentence. The length of the sentence must reflect the seriousness of the offence, although longer sentences—within the statutory maxima—may be imposed on violent and sexual offenders.

Average sentence length in England and Wales in 1994 for principal offences at the Crown Court for males aged 21 and over sentenced for indictable offences

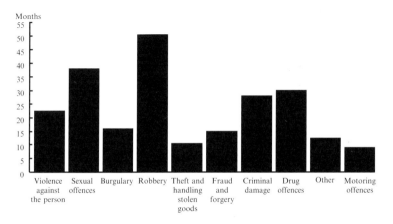

Source: *Criminal Statistics England and Wales 1994.*

A magistrates' court cannot impose a term of more than six months' imprisonment for an individual offence tried summarily. It can impose consecutive sentences for 'either way' offences, subject to an overall maximum of 12 months' imprisonment. If an offence carries a higher maximum penalty, the court may commit the offender for sentence at the Crown Court. The Crown Court may impose a custodial sentence for any term up to life, depending on the seriousness of the offence and the maximum penalty available.

If a court decides that an offence is sufficiently serious to justify an immediate custodial sentence of not more than two years, the sentence may be suspended for a period of at least one year and not more than two years if exceptional circumstances justify the suspension. If the offender commits another imprisonable offence during the period of suspension, the court may order the suspended sentence to be served in addition to any punishment imposed for the second offence. When passing a suspended sentence, the court must consider whether it would also be appropriate to impose a fine or make a compensation order. The court may also order supervision of the offender by a probation officer if the suspended sentence is for more than six months.

There is a mandatory sentence of life imprisonment for murder throughout Britain. Life imprisonment is the maximum penalty for a number of serious offences, such as robbery, rape, arson and manslaughter.

Northern Ireland

In Northern Ireland the position is generally the same as for England and Wales. A magistrates' court, however, cannot commit an offender for sentencing at the Crown Court if it has tried the case.

Scotland

In Scottish trials on indictment the High Court of Justiciary may impose a sentence of imprisonment for any term up to life, and the sheriff court any term up to three years. The latter may send any person to the High Court for sentence if the court considers its powers are insufficient. In summary cases the sheriff or stipendiary magistrate may normally impose up to three months' imprisonment or six months' for some repeated offences. The district court can impose a maximum term of imprisonment of 60 days.

The Death Penalty

The death penalty remains on the statute book for the offences of treason, piracy with violence and some other treasonable and mutinous offences. It has, however, not been used for any of these offences since 1946.

Non-custodial Treatment

Non-custodial sentences include:

—fines;

—compensation orders;

—probation and supervision orders;

—community service orders;

—a combination order, which includes elements of probation and community service;

—a supervised attendance order (Scotland only—see p. 68); and

—a supervised release order (Scotland only—see p. 74).

Fines

About 80 per cent of offenders are punished with a fine. There is no limit to the fine, unless set by statute, which the Crown Court may impose on indictment; this also applies to fines imposed by the High Court of Justiciary and the sheriff court in Scotland under solemn procedure. The maximum fine that can be imposed by a magistrates' court in England and Wales is normally £5,000, although many summary offences carry lower maxima. In Scotland this is also the maximum fine that can be imposed by the sheriff court under summary procedure; the maximum fine in district court cases is £2,500. When fixing the amount of a fine, courts are required to reflect the seriousness of the offence and to take into account the financial circumstances of the offender.

Probation

The locally organised probation service in England and Wales supervises offenders in the community under direct court orders and after release from custody. It also provides offenders in custody with help and advice.

A court probation order can last between six months and three years; if the offender fails to comply with any of the requirements of the order, he or she can be brought before the court again. A probation order can be combined with a community service order.

A probation order requires the offender to maintain regular contact with the probation officer, who is expected to supervise the offender and to confront him or her with the consequences of the offence. An offender may have to report weekly for the first three months, then fortnightly and, if all is going well, every three to four weeks.

Special conditions attached to the order may require the offender to attend a day centre for up to 60 days. Probation is a punishment, although the time spent by offenders under supervision in the community offers an opportunity for constructive work to reduce the likelihood of reoffending.

In England and Wales the probation service also administers supervision orders (see p. 84), the community service scheme and supervises those released from prison on parole (see p. 73). The service aims to ensure that community sentences provide a tough and demanding punishment which is effective in reducing further offending.

The statutory Probation Inspectorate monitors the work of the voluntary and private sectors with the probation service in addition to its inspection and advisory duties.

In Scotland local authority social work departments supervise offenders on probation, community service and other community disposals, and offenders subject to supervision on release from custody.

In Northern Ireland the service is administered by the government-funded Probation Board, whose membership is representative of the community.

Community Service

Offenders aged 16 or over convicted of imprisonable offences may, with their consent, be given community service orders. The court may order between 40 and 240 hours' unpaid service to be completed within 12 months. Examples of work done include decorating the houses of elderly or disabled people and building adventure playgrounds. Community service punishes offenders by making them do work and give something back to the community.

In England and Wales the court may make an order combining community service and probation. The maximum term for the probation element is the same as a probation order and the maximum period of community service is 100 hours (240 hours in Scotland).

Curfew Order

The Criminal Justice and Public Order Act 1994 provides for the use of curfew orders with electronic monitoring in trial areas. Courts in the trial areas can require offenders to remain at home for periods of between two and 12 hours a day. The order can be combined with probation or community service. A decision on whether to extend the order to courts throughout England and Wales will be taken in the light of the trials.

Compensation

The courts may order an offender to pay compensation for personal injury, loss or damage resulting from an offence. In England and Wales courts are required to give reasons for not awarding compensation to a victim. Compensation takes precedence over fines.

Other Measures

A court in England and Wales may discharge a person either absolutely or conditionally if it believes that it is not necessary to inflict punishment. If he or she is conditionally discharged, the offender remains liable to punishment for the offence if convicted of another offence within a period specified by the court (not more than three years).

Courts may also require an offender to keep the peace and/or be of good behaviour. If this requirement is not complied with, the offender is liable to forfeit a sum of money. Similar powers are available to courts in Northern Ireland.

Courts have the power to defer sentence, for the purpose of enabling the court, in dealing with the offender subsequently, to have regard to his or her conduct or any change in his or her circumstances.

In Scotland, supervised attendance order schemes have been piloted in a number of areas. These schemes provide an alternative to imprisonment for fine default, and incorporate aspects of work and training. New legislation is extending their use to form an alternative in the first instance to fines for young offenders.

The police have discretion whether to charge an offender or formally to caution him or her. Cautioning is a form of warning and no court action is taken. Properly used, it is an effective deterrent to those who have committed minor offences or who have offended for the first time. However, it is an inappropriate response to serious offences; new guidelines designed to stop the use of cautions for such offences and to cut the number of repeated cautions were issued by the Government in 1994. Cautioning is not available in Scotland.

Government Proposals
In March 1995 the Government published for consultation proposals for a single, integrated community sentence in England and Wales to replace existing community punishments. The proposed new sentence, clarifying the purpose of a community sentence, would give the courts greater choice of community penalties and more say over the type of supervision or work the offender must carry out. The Government also proposed to review the current community sentences available for young offenders and to abolish the requirement that offenders give consent for some community orders.

Prisons

The goals of the Prison Service in England and Wales are to:

—maintain order, control, discipline and a safe environment;

—provide decent but austere conditions for prisoners and meet their needs, including health care;

—provide positive regimes which help prisoners address their offending behaviour and allow them as full and responsible a life as possible;

—help prisoners prepare for their return to the community; and

—deliver prison services using the resources provided by Parliament with maximum efficiency.

Scotland and Northern Ireland have separate prison services run by the Scottish and Northern Ireland Offices. The Prison Service in England and Wales and the Scottish Prison Service became executive agencies in April 1993. The Northern Ireland Prison Service became an executive agency in April 1995. Government ministers remain accountable for policy but the Chief Executives are responsible for the delivery of services.

There are about 130 prison establishments in England and Wales and 22 in Scotland, many of which were built in the 19th century. There has been a major refurbishment and prison building programme in England and Wales over recent years, leading to a substantial improvement in prison conditions and the alleviation of overcrowding. Over 95 per cent of prisoners in England and Wales now have access to sanitation at all times, compared to 46 per cent in 1981.

In Northern Ireland there are four prisons and a young offenders' centre. Four of these establishments have been built since 1972.

Since 1991 the Government has been implementing a programme of reforms for the prison service in England and Wales and in Scotland. It is designed to provide a better prison system, with more effective measures for control, more constructive relationships between prisoners and staff, and more stimulating and useful programmes for prisoners.

Prisoner Classification

The average prison population in 1994 was 48,800 in England and Wales, 1,920 in Northern Ireland, and 5,600 in Scotland. Prisoners may be housed in accommodation ranging from open prisons to high-security establishments. In England and Wales sentenced prisoners are classified into four groups for security purposes:

—Category A for those whose escape would be highly dangerous to the public, the police or the security of the state;

—Category B for those for whom escape must be made very difficult;

—Category C for prisoners who cannot be trusted in open conditions but who do not have the will or resource to make a determined escape attempt; or

—Category D for those who can be trusted to serve their sentence in open conditions.

Similar classifications exist in the Scottish Prison Service.

There are separate prisons for women. There are no open prisons in Northern Ireland, where the majority of offenders are serving sentences for terrorist offences. People awaiting trial in custody are entitled to privileges not granted to convicted prisoners. Those under 21 are, where possible, separated from convicted prisoners.

In 1995–96 the key priority of the Prison Service in England and Wales is to strengthen physical security and security procedures, particularly at establishments holding high-security prisoners.

Private Sector Involvement

Under the Criminal Justice Act 1991, the Home Secretary is empowered to contract out the management of prisons in England and Wales to the private sector, as well as escort and guarding functions.

The Court Escort and Custody Service is being progressively contracted out throughout the country. All escort services will be provided by the private sector by 1997 leaving police and prison officers free to concentrate on their own core duties.

Four prisons (which remain part of the Prison Service) are now managed by private contractors. The Wolds in Humberside opened in April 1992, Blakenhurst prison in Worcestershire opened in May 1993, and Doncaster prison and Buckley Hall prison in Rochdale opened in June and December 1994 respectively.

The Government has announced that six new prisons to be built will, for the first time, be designed, constructed, managed and financed by the private sector. The first two are expected to open in 1997–98 in Merseyside and South Wales.

The Prison Service is also continuing to contract out services both nationally and locally, including education services in prison and catering. Provision for the further contracting out of prisons and prisoner escort services is included in the Criminal Justice and Public Order Act 1994.

Unconvicted Prisoners

Some of the prison population consists of unconvicted prisoners held in custody and awaiting trial. These prisoners are presumed to be innocent and are treated accordingly. They are allowed all reasonable facilities to seek release on bail, prepare for trial, maintain contact with relatives and friends, and pursue legitimate business and social interests. They also have the right to wear their own clothes and can write and receive unlimited numbers of letters.

Early Release of Prisoners
England and Wales

The Criminal Justice Act 1991 reformed the remission and parole systems in England and Wales, with revised arrangements for the early release of prisoners and for their supervision and liabilities after release. The Parole Board continues to advise the Home Secretary, who retains formal responsibility, on the early release or recall of long-term prisoners.

Prisoners serving terms of less than four years may be released once they have served half of their sentences in custody, subject to good prison behaviour. Long-term prisoners (those serving more than four years) may be released once they have served two-thirds of their sentence; the Parole Board may release them on licence half-way through their sentence if they are serving between four and seven years. The Home Secretary has to give final consent to such parole if the prisoner is serving more than seven years. All prisoners sentenced to a year or more may be supervised on release until three-quarters of their sentence has passed. Certain sex offenders may be supervised to the end of their sentence.

If convicted of another offence punishable with imprisonment and committed before the end of the original sentence, a released prisoner may be liable to serve all or part of the original sentence outstanding at the time the fresh offence was committed. Under the 1991 legislation in England and Wales, a prisoner can be released on exceptional compassionate grounds at any time during the sentence. Release in these circumstances is on licence to the end of the sentence.

Scotland

Under the Prisoners and Criminal Proceedings (Scotland) Act 1993, prisoners serving terms of less than four years are released once they have served half of their sentence, and are not subject to supervision in the community. Prisoners serving longer terms may be released after half of their sentence at the discretion of the Parole Board for Scotland, and will be released after two-thirds of their sentence. Such prisoners are subject to supervision on release by local authority social work departments until the full sentence is completed. In addition, courts may impose a supervised release order at time of sentence on offenders due to serve terms of less than four years, which will result in supervision for a period of up to 12 months on release.

If a prisoner released subject to supervision commits an offence punishable with imprisonment before the end of the original sentence, he or she may be liable to serve all or part of the original sentence outstanding at the time of the offence in addition to any sentence for the new offence. In such cases, release will be subject to supervision even when the term served is less than four years.

Northern Ireland

In Northern Ireland prisoners serving a sentence of more than five days are eligible for remission of half their sentence. A prisoner serving a sentence of more than 12 months who is given remission is liable to be ordered to serve the remainder of this sentence if convicted of fresh imprisonable offences during this period.

Remission for those convicted of terrorist offences and serving sentences of five years or more is one-third. Any released prisoners convicted of another terrorist offence before the expiry of the original sentence must complete that sentence before serving any term for the second offence.

Life Sentence Prisoners

Arrangements for the early release of prisoners in England and Wales serving life sentences for offences other than murder are set out in the Criminal Justice Act 1991. When such a life sentence is passed, the judge specifies in open court a period of time after which the prisoner is entitled to have his or her case referred to the Parole Board. Once that period expires, the Board reviews the case and orders the prisoner's release if it is satisfied that he or she is no longer a risk to the public.

The Parole Board panel, which considers these cases, is chaired by a judge and adopts a judicial procedure, under which the prisoner is entitled to put his or her case and be legally represented.

Prisoners sentenced prior to the beginning of October 1992, when the new procedures came into force, are also eligible if they are so certified by the Home Secretary.

The changes were introduced to comply with judgments made by the European Court of Human Rights. Similar procedures exist in Scotland.

These changes in the law do not affect prisoners serving mandatory life sentences for murder. In England and Wales the release on licence of prisoners serving mandatory life sentences for murder may be authorised only by the Home Secretary on the recommendation of the Parole Board. A similar policy applies in Scotland.

Those serving life sentences for the murder of police and prison officers, terrorist murders, murder by firearms in the course of robbery and the sexual or sadistic murder of children are normally detained for at least 20 years.

On release, all life sentence prisoners remain on licence for the rest of their lives and are subject to recall should their behaviour suggest that they might again be a danger to the public.

In Northern Ireland all life sentence cases are reviewed regularly by a Life Sentence Review Board after ten years of imprisonment and on occasions earlier. If the Board is satisfied that a prisoner fulfils criteria for release, a recommendation is made to government ministers, and the views of the judiciary are sought. The Board may recommend release or a further review in one to five years' time. The Secretary of State takes the final decision to release a life-sentence prisoner under licence.

Repatriation

Sentenced prisoners who are nationals of countries which have ratified the Council of Europe Convention on the Transfer of Sentenced Persons or similar international arrangements may apply to be returned to their own country to serve the rest of their sentence there.

Independent Oversight of the Prison System

Every prison establishment has a Board of Visitors—a Visiting Committee in Scotland—drawn from the local community, which acts as a watchdog for the Secretary of State. These bodies oversee prison administration and the treatment of prisoners. In order to see that prisoners are being treated fairly, members may go to any part of the prison and interview any inmate at any time.

The independent Prisons Inspectorates report to the respective Secretaries of State on the treatment of prisoners and prison conditions. Each establishment is visited about every three years. Reports of full (announced) and short (unannounced) inspections are published. The Inspectorates submit annual reports to Parliament.

Prison Industries

Prison industries aim to give inmates work experience which will assist them when released and to secure a financial return which will reduce the cost of the prison system. The main industries are clothing and textile manufacture, engineering, woodwork, laundering, farming and horticulture. In England and Wales most production caters for internal needs and for other public services, whereas in Scotland a greater proportion is sold to the private sector. A few prisoners are employed outside prison, some in community service projects.

Prison Education

Education of 15 hours a week is compulsory for young offenders below school leaving age. For older offenders it is voluntary. Some prisoners study for public examinations, including those of the Open University. Competitive tendering for the provision of education services in prisons in England and Wales has taken place and contracts have been awarded, many to further and higher education establishments. In England, Wales and Scotland increased emphasis is being placed on the development and implementation of National and Scottish Vocational Qualifications for inmates.

Physical education is voluntary for adult offenders but compulsory for young offenders. Practically all prisons have physical education facilities, some of which are purpose-built. Opportunities are given for inmates to obtain sporting proficiency awards. Inmates also compete against teams in the local community.

Health Care

The Health Care Service for Prisoners in England and Wales is responsible for the physical and mental health of all those in custody. A Health Advisory Committee provides independent medical advice to government ministers, the Prison Service Chief Executive and the Director of Health Care.

A greater emphasis is being placed on 'buying in' health care services either from the National Health Service (NHS) or the private sector. The Prison Service is also committed to transferring mentally disordered offenders to the care and treatment of the NHS and social services where possible.

In Scotland general medical services are provided mainly by visiting general practitioners. Psychiatric and psychological services are bought in from local health boards responsible for the NHS.

Privileges and Discipline

Prisoners may write and receive letters and be visited by relatives and friends, and those in all establishments in England, Wales and Scotland may make telephone calls. Privileges include a personal radio, books, periodicals and newspapers, watching television, and the opportunity to make purchases from the prison shop with money earned in prison. Depending on facilities available, prisoners may be granted the further privileges of dining and recreation in association.

In Northern Ireland all prisoners can wear their own clothes. Convicted prisoners may have weekly visits in open conditions with families and friends, while those awaiting trial may have up to three such visits a week.

To maintain discipline, control and order the Prison Service in England and Wales is:

—developing incentive-based regimes, so that prisoners must earn privileges through responsible behaviour and will lose them for misbehaviour;

—increasing the penalties available to governors to deal with disciplinary offences;

—providing special units with facilities for dealing with violent or disruptive prisoners; and

—implementing a comprehensive strategy on drug misuse, including mandatory urine testing.

Breaches of discipline are dealt with by the prison governor. A Prisons Ombudsman for England and Wales has been appointed as a final appeal stage for prisoners' grievances.

In Scotland, prisoners who exhaust the internal grievance procedure may make application to the Scottish Prisons Complaints Commission, which is independent of the Scottish Prison Service.

Prisoners are allowed to write to their Member of Parliament, to petition Parliament, to contact their Member of the European Parliament and to apply to the European Commission of Human

Rights. General letters about the penal system may also be sent to newspapers and to the producers of television and radio programmes.

Women Prisoners

Women prisoners in England and Wales do not wear prison uniform and there is a clothing allowance to help pay for clothes while in prison. The Prison Services in England and Wales and in Scotland have mother and baby units, which enable babies to remain with their mothers where that is found to be in the best interests of the child. In addition to the usual visiting arrangements, several prisons allow extended visits to enable women to spend a whole day with their children in an informal atmosphere.

Ethnic Minority Prisoners

The Prison Services have public policy statements about race relations, which have to be clearly displayed in every prison. These say that the Service is committed to a policy of racial equality and to the elimination of discrimination in all aspects of its work. It is a disciplinary offence for a prison officer to use racially abusive language.

Each prison has a race relations liaison officer, who deals with complaints from prisoners about racial discrimination and with problems or queries of a racial nature. A prisoner can also complain to the Commission for Racial Equality.

Welfare

Prison officers deal with welfare matters and are supported in this by probation staff (in Scotland, social workers). Prison probation officers give help and advice with personal and domestic problems, such as outstanding debt, relationships and problems with visits. They also help to prepare prisoners for release by:

— helping them with arrangements for temporary licence;

— putting them in touch with probation officers outside prison; and

— contacting other outside bodies which may be able to offer help in arranging accommodation, training, education or employment.

Religion

Anglican, Church of Scotland, Roman Catholic and Methodist chaplains provide opportunities for worship and spiritual counselling. They are supported by visiting ministers of other denominations and faiths as required.

Preparation for Release

The Prison Services in England and Wales and in Scotland have a duty to prepare prisoners for release. Planning for safe release begins at the start of an offender's sentence and ties in with all the training, education and work experience provided. It is directed at equipping prisoners to reintegrate into society and to cope with life without re-offending. Risk assessment and confronting offending behaviour are essential elements of this process. Sentence planning is being extended progressively to all prisoners serving substantial sentences, in conjunction with extended arrangements for after-care.

Prisoners in England and Wales may be granted temporary licence for short periods, but they are subject to a rigorous risk assessment and are released only for very specific reasons. Temporary licence may be granted:

—on specific compassionate grounds (compassionate licence);

—towards the end of a sentence to help prisoners in re-integrating into the community (resettlement licence); and

—for education, training or work experience to help in prisoner rehabilitation (but not for category A or B prisoners or where suitable courses are available in prison), and for specific official purposes, such as to appear as police witnesses (facility licence).

There are similar arrangements for temporary release in Scotland.

Any prisoner released temporarily from prison who fails to return on expiry of his licence is liable to further criminal charges.

The Pre-Release Employment Scheme in England and Wales and the Training for Freedom Scheme in Scotland enable selected long-term prisoners to spend their last six months before release in certain hostels attached to prisons, to help them re-adapt to society. Hostellers work in the outside community and return to the hostel each evening. Weekend leave allows hostellers to renew ties with their families.

In Northern Ireland prisoners serving fixed sentences may have short periods of leave near the end of their sentences and at Christmas. Life-sentence prisoners are given a nine-month pre-release programme, which includes employment outside the prison.

Aftercare

Professional social work support is given to offenders following their release to help them adjust on their return to society. Since the entry into force of the Criminal Justice Act 1991 in England and Wales, all young offenders and all adult offenders sentenced to 12 months' imprisonment and over are supervised on release by the probation service—or, in the case of certain young offenders by local authority social services departments. In Scotland this support is provided by local authority social work services, although not all adult offenders are subject to supervision on release (see p. 74)

Assistance is also provided by independent organisations. This ranges from the provision of accommodation for ex-offenders to advice on education, training and employment. The Home Office helps fund this work through grants to the organisations, which include the National Association for the Care and Resettlement of Offenders (NACRO). Other organisations work on a local level in partnership with the probation service.

In Scotland a similar range of organisations are involved.

Prison Reform

There are a number of independent organisations like NACRO which campaign for improved prison conditions and the greater use of alternatives to custody. The Prison Reform Trust, for instance, publishes a guide for prisoners about their rights; this is produced jointly with the Prison Service for England and Wales. The Howard League for Penal Reform campaigns for a more humane criminal justice system and assists prisoners and their families. The National Prisoners' Movement handles enquiries from prisoners and their families from an ex-prisoner viewpoint and provides legal back-up. JUSTICE is an organisation concerned with law reform and helps prisoners by investigating cases where there is a valid complaint about conviction or sentence.

Young Offenders

England and Wales

Criminal proceedings cannot be brought against children below the age of 10 years. Offenders between the ages of 10 and 18 fall within the jurisdiction of youth courts. Sixteen- and 17-year-olds may be given the same probation, curfew and community service orders as older offenders. Also available to the court are supervision orders or attendance centre orders.

Supervision Orders

Under a supervision order—which may remain in force for not more than three years—a child (10–13 years old) or young person (14–17 years old) normally lives at home under the supervision of a social worker or a probation officer. The order may require the offender to live in local authority accommodation and/or participate in specified activities at specified times.

Attendance Centres

Anyone under 21 years of age found guilty of an offence for which an adult may be imprisoned can be ordered to go to an attendance centre, as can an offender who refuses to comply with another order (for example, default in paying a fine or breach of a probation order). The maximum number of hours of attendance is 36 (or 24 if the offender is aged under 16) spread over a period; the minimum is 12 hours, although where the offender is under 14 years of age the court has a discretion to impose a lesser total. The order aims to encourage offenders to make more constructive use of their leisure time.

Detention

Crown Court powers to order long periods of detention for young offenders who commit serious crimes are extended under the provisions of the Criminal Justice and Public Order Act 1994 to include 10- to 13-year-olds. The courts may detain 10- to 13-year-olds convicted of an offence for which an adult can be jailed for 14 years or more (including rape, arson, domestic burglary and robbery). Previously they could be given long terms of detention only if they had been convicted of murder or manslaughter.

Courts may also detain any 10- to 15-year-old convicted of indecent assault on a woman, where previously only 16- and 17-year-olds could be detained for this offence. Any offender aged 14 or over who is convicted of causing death by dangerous or drunken driving may also be detained. Detention may be in a local authority secure residential unit, a centre managed by the Youth Treatment Service or a young offender institution.

The basic custodial sentence for those aged 15 to 21 is detention in a young offender institution. Alternatives include fines and compensation, attendance centre orders (for up to 36 hours) and community service orders (for between 40 and 240 hours).

Criminal Justice and Public Order Act 1994

In the area of parental responsibility, the Criminal Justice and Public Order Act 1994 extends the powers given to the courts by the Criminal Justice Act 1991. The 1991 Act:

—strengthened courts' powers to make parents attend hearings in cases involving offenders up to the age of 18;

—strengthened the liability on parents to pay fines and compensation arising from the crimes committed by their children;

—contained greater power for courts to order parents to take proper care and control of their children if necessary to prevent further offences; and

—allowed such orders to be imposed for up to three years, or until the offender's 18th birthday.

Where local authorities have assumed parental responsibility, the duty to attend court and pay any fines also applies.

Under the 1994 legislation, courts can order parents to ensure their children comply with community sentences. In every case when an offender aged between 10 and 15 years receives a community sentence, the court is under a duty to consider such an order. Courts have a power, as opposed to a duty, in the case of 16- and 17-year-olds.

Courts are also empowered to impose a secure training order on persistent offenders aged between 12 and 14. The order means a period of detention in a secure training centre followed by a period of supervision; it is available for young offenders who have committed three or more imprisonable offences and who have failed to respond to punishment in the community. A further provision doubles the maximum sentence for 15- to 17-year-olds in a young offender institution from one to two years.

Scotland

Criminal proceedings may be brought against any child aged eight years or over, but the instructions of the Lord Advocate are necessary before anyone under 16 years of age is prosecuted.

Children under 16 who have committed an offence or are considered to be in need of care and protection may be brought before a children's panel. The panel, consisting of three lay people, determines in an informal setting whether compulsory measures of care

are required and, if so, the form they should take. An official known as the reporter decides whether a child should come before a hearing. If the grounds for referral are not accepted by the child or parent, the case goes to the sheriff for proof. If he or she finds the grounds established, the sheriff remits the case to the reporter to arrange a hearing. The sheriff also decides appeals against a hearing's decision.

Custody in a young offender institution is available to the criminal courts for young people aged between 16 and 21. Remission of part of the sentence for good behaviour, release on parole and supervision on release are available.

Northern Ireland
Those aged between 10 and 16 who are charged with a criminal offence are normally brought before a juvenile court. If found guilty of an offence punishable in the case of an adult by imprisonment, the court may order the offender to be placed in care, under supervision or on probation. The offender may also be required to attend a day attendance centre, be sent to a training school or committed to residence in a remand home. Non-custodial options are the same as in England and Wales.

Offenders aged between 16 and 24 who receive custodial sentences of less than three years serve them in a young offenders' centre.

Administration of the Law

Government Responsibilities

Administration of justice rests with the Lord Chancellor, the Lord Advocate, the Home Secretary, the Attorney General and the Secretaries of State for Scotland and Northern Ireland. The highest judicial appointments are made by the Queen on the advice of the Prime Minister. The judiciary is independent, its adjudications not being subject to ministerial direction or control.

England and Wales

The Lord Chancellor is head of the judiciary and is responsible for:

—appointing most magistrates;

—recommending and advising on the appointment of the senior judiciary;

—the procedure of the magistrates' courts;

—the administration of magistrates' and higher courts; and

—the legal aid and advice schemes.

The Home Secretary is concerned with the criminal law, the police service, prisons, and the probation and after-care service. He appoints a Board of Visitors to each prison establishment (see p. 76), and is advised by the Parole Board on the release of prisoners on licence. The Home Secretary is also responsible for advising the Queen on the exercise of the Royal Prerogative of Mercy.

The Attorney General and the Solicitor General are the Government's principal advisers on English law, and they represent the Crown in appropriate domestic and international cases. They are senior barristers and elected members of the House of Commons and hold ministerial posts. The Attorney General has final responsibility for enforcing the criminal law. The Solicitor General is the deputy of the Attorney General. As head of the Crown Prosecution Service, the Director of Public Prosecutions is subject to superintendence by the Attorney General, as are the Director of the Serious Fraud Office and the Director of Public Prosecutions for Northern Ireland.

Scotland

The Secretary of State for Scotland is responsible for the criminal law of Scotland, crime prevention, the police, the penal system and legal aid; he or she is advised on parole matters by the Parole Board for Scotland.

The Secretary of State recommends the appointment of all judges other than the most senior ones, appoints the staff of the High Court of Justiciary, and is responsible, through the Scottish Courts Service, for the composition, staffing and organisation of the sheriff courts. District courts are staffed and administered by the district and islands local authorities.

The Lord Advocate and the Solicitor General for Scotland are the chief legal advisers to the Government on Scottish questions and the principal representatives of the Crown for the purposes of prosecutions and other litigation in Scotland. Both are government ministers. The Lord Advocate is responsible for evidential policy and is closely concerned with legal policy and administration; he or she is also responsible for the Scottish parliamentary counsel who draft Scottish legislation.

Northern Ireland

The administration of all courts is the responsibility of the Lord Chancellor, while the Northern Ireland Office, under the Secretary of State, deals with the criminal law, the police and the penal system. The Attorney General for England and Wales is also Attorney General for Northern Ireland. The Lord Chancellor has general responsibility for legal aid, advice and assistance.

The Personnel of the Law

Judges

Judges are normally appointed from practising barristers, (advocates in Scotland) or solicitors (see below).

High Court judges, circuit judges and recorders are appointed by the Queen on the recommendation of the Lord Chancellor. District judges are appointed by the Lord Chancellor. Circuit judges and district judges are appointed through a competitive procedure including an interview before a panel which makes recommendations to the Lord Chancellor. Over the next few years, this procedure for making appointments is to be extended to all judicial posts below the level of the High Court.

Circuit judges, who preside in county courts and the Crown Court, are appointed from barristers or solicitors who have held a right of audience in the Crown Court or county courts for at least ten years or from recorders with at least two years' experience. Recorders are part-time judges in the Crown Court and county courts and are appointed from among those barristers or solicitors who have held a right of audience in the Crown Court or county courts for at least ten years; they are expected to sit for at least 20 days a year but no more than 50. High Court judges are appointed from practitioners who have held a right of audience in the High Court for at least ten years, or from among circuit judges who have served for at least two years.

Court of Appeal judges are appointed by the Queen on the recommendation of the Prime Minister, usually from among High Court judges. The Law Lords (in the House of Lords) are usually appointed from among Court of Appeal judges or the Scottish equivalent.

In Scotland, Supreme Court judges, sheriffs principal and sheriffs are appointed by the Queen on the recommendation of the Secretary of State for Scotland. They are chosen from advocates or solicitors who have had many years' experience as practitioners in the Supreme or sheriff courts.

Lay magistrates in England and Wales (see p. 41) need no legal qualifications but receive training so that they have sufficient knowledge of the law, including the rules of evidence, and of the nature and purpose of sentencing.

The Scottish district court justices of the peace need no legal qualifications, but they too must take part in training. Stipendiary magistrates (see p. 56) are legally qualified.

In Northern Ireland all full-time judges and resident magistrates are appointed by the Queen and are drawn from the legal profession. Members of a lay panel who serve in juvenile courts undertake training courses.

The Legal Profession

The legal profession is divided into two branches: barristers (advocates in Scotland) and solicitors. Barristers and advocates advise on legal problems submitted through solicitors or other recognised professional bodies and present cases in all courts. Solicitors undertake legal business for individual and corporate clients; they can also, after appropriate training, present cases in all courts. Although people are free to conduct their own cases, most people prefer to be legally represented, especially in more serious cases.

Barristers belong to one of the four Inns of Court in England and Wales—Lincoln's Inn, Gray's Inn, the Inner Temple and the Middle Temple—or the Inn of Court of Northern Ireland. Students study in the Inns of Court School of Law and must complete satisfactorily the skills-based course before being called to the Bar. They must then serve an apprenticeship with a qualified barrister for one year. Barristers must be members of the General Council of the Bar, which upholds professional standards and has certain disciplinary powers. The corresponding body in Scotland is the Faculty of Advocates.

Professional examinations must also be passed before anyone can become a solicitor. After that, a two-year period of work experience, called a training contract, is served in a solicitor's office. Once qualified in this way, a newly admitted solicitor is supervised for a period of three years. The Law Society in England and Wales is the governing body of the profession and has disciplinary powers over practising solicitors. It also regulates admission, education and training. A solicitor is bound contractually to his or her client and can be sued for negligence. In Scotland the Law Society of Scotland represents solicitors. The governing body in Northern Ireland is the Law Society of Northern Ireland.

Complaints systems against solicitors, barristers and licensed conveyancers are backed up by the Legal Services Ombudsman for England and Wales, who conducts investigations into the way the professional bodies handle these complaints. There is a separate Ombudsman for Scotland.

Legal Aid in Criminal Proceedings

England and Wales

A person who needs legal advice or legal representation in court may be able to get help with his or her legal costs from the legal aid scheme. A person who qualifies for help may have all his or her legal costs paid for, or may be asked to pay a contribution towards them, depending on his or her means.

If the police question a person about an offence—whether or not he or she has been arrested—he or she has the right to free legal advice from a solicitor. If the person has to go to the magistrates' court on a criminal case, there is usually a duty solicitor available at the court or on call to give free legal advice and representation when the defendant appears in court for the first time.

Anyone charged with a criminal offence may apply for criminal legal aid. Criminal legal aid covers solicitors' costs for preparing the defence and representing a person in court; if a barrister is needed, this is also covered. It also covers advice on appeal against a verdict or sentence of the magistrates' court or the Crown Court and preparing the notice of appeal. It may also be available for bail application.

Applications for criminal legal aid are made to the court where the case is to be heard. The court supplies the necessary application forms, which are filled in by the applicant or his or her solicitor.

Applicants are asked to give details of their income and capital, including savings.

The court is responsible for deciding whether legal aid should be granted. Its decision is based on the information given by the defendant in the application form for legal aid and the form detailing the defendant's means. The court will grant a defendant legal aid if it decides that it is in the interests of justice that he or she should be legally represented, and that he or she needs help in meeting the costs of the case.

The court may decide that it is in the interests of justice to grant criminal legal aid if, for example:

— the case is so serious that, if found guilty, the defendant could go to prison or lose his/her job or suffer serious damage to his/her reputation;

— there are substantial questions of law to be argued; or

— the defendant is unable to follow the proceedings or explain his or her case, because he or she does not speak English well, or is mentally ill.

If the court refuses to grant legal aid, an applicant may be able to apply to have the case reviewed by an area committee of the Legal Aid Board. Otherwise the defendant must reapply to the court. There is no limit to the number of applications that can be made to the court for legal aid, and this can be done at any time up to the trial itself.

If legal aid is granted, the defendant may be asked to pay a contribution towards costs, depending on his or her income and savings.

Scotland

Legal aid in Scottish criminal proceedings is available to all persons in custody on their first appearance in the sheriff courts and the district courts without enquiry into the person's means. Thereafter (or if the person has been cited to attend the court and is not in custody) a person seeking legal aid must apply to the Scottish Legal Aid Board. The Board assesses all applications for legal aid in summary criminal cases and must be satisfied that the costs of the case cannot be met by the applicant without undue hardship, and that it is in the interests of justice that legal aid is awarded.

In solemn proceedings the court determines whether legal aid is to be available and must be satisfied only that the accused cannot meet the costs of the defence without undue financial hardship. Where legal aid is granted in criminal proceedings to the accused, he or she is not required to pay any contribution towards expenses.

Northern Ireland

Legal aid for criminal cases in Northern Ireland is free; it is allocated if the court is satisfied that the defendant's means are such that it is in the interests of justice that legal aid should be granted. There is a voluntary duty solicitor scheme at the principal magistrates' court in Belfast.

Addresses

Criminal Injuries Compensation Board, 19 Alfred Place, London WC1E 7EA.

Crown Office, Regent Road, Edinburgh EH7 5BC.

Crown Prosecution Service, 50 Ludgate Hill, London EC4M 7EX.

General Council of the Bar, 3 Bedford Row, London WC1R 4DB.

Home Office, 50 Queen Anne's Gate, London SW1H 9AT.

Howard League for Penal Reform, 322 Kennington Park Road, London SE11 4PP.

Independent Commission for Police Complaints for Northern Ireland, 22 Great Victoria Street, Belfast BT2 7LP.

JUSTICE, 95a Chancery Lane, London WC2A 2DT.

Law Society, 50 Chancery Lane, London WC2A 1SX.

Law Society of Northern Ireland, 90–106 Victoria Street, Belfast BT1 3JZ.

Law Society of Scotland, 26–28 Drumsheugh Gardens, Edinburgh EH3 7YR.

Legal Aid Board, 29-37 Red Lion Street, London WC1R 4PP.

Legal Secretariat to the Law Officers, Attorney General's Chambers, 9 Buckingham Gate, London SW1E 6JP.

Liberty, 21 Tabard Street, London SE1 4LA.

Lord Chancellor's Office, Trevelyan House, 30 Great Peter Street, London SW1P 2BY.

Metropolitan Police Service, New Scotland Yard, Broadway, London SW1H 0BG.

National Association for the Care and Resettlement of Offenders, 169 Clapham Road, London SW9 0PU.

Northern Ireland Information Service, Stormont Castle, Belfast BT4 3ST.

Police Complaints Authority, 10 Great George Street, London SW1P 3AE.

Scottish Association for the Care and Resettlement of Offenders, 53 George Street, Edinburgh EH2 2ET.

Scottish Legal Aid Board, 44 Drumsheugh Gardens, Edinburgh EH3 7SW.

Scottish Office Information Directorate, New St Andrew's House, Edinburgh EH1 3TG.

Serious Fraud Office, Elm House, Elm Street, London WC1X 0BJ.

Further Reading

Annual Reports

Annual reports are published by the following:

Criminal Injuries Compensation Board

Crown Office and Procurator Fiscal Service

Crown Prosecution Service

Her Majesty's Chief Inspector of Constabulary

Her Majesty's Chief Inspector of Constabulary for Scotland

Her Majesty's Chief Inspector of Prisons

Her Majesty's Prison Service

Lord Chancellor's Department Court Service

Metropolitan Police Commissioner

Northern Ireland Prison Service

Police Complaints Authority

Serious Fraud Office

Statistics

Criminal Statistics England and Wales

Lord Chancellor's Department Judicial Statistics

Prison Statistics England and Wales

Index

Printed in the UK for HMSO.
Dd.0301578, 12/95, C30, 56–6734, 5673.